Human Reproduction, Contraception, Family Planning and Sex

Kuldeep Kaushik

Foreword by

Laxmi Kanta Chawla
Health & Family Welfare Minister, Punjab

PEACOCK BOOKS

Published by
PEACOCK BOOKS
7/22, Ansari Road, Darya Ganj,
New Delhi-110002
Phones : +91-11-40775252, 23273880, 23275880, 23280451
Fax : +91-11-23285873
Web : www.atlanticbooks.com
E-mail : info@atlanticbooks.com

Branch Office
5, Nallathambi Street, Wallajah Road,
Chennai-600002
Phones : +91-44-64611085, 32413319
E-mail : chennai@atlanticbooks.com

Peacock Books is an imprint of
Atlantic Publishers and Distributors (P) Ltd

Printed in India at Nice Printing Press, A-33/3A, Site-IV,
Industrial Area, Sahibabad, Ghaziabad, U.P.

It is a little contribution towards the initiative which was taken by my supervisors

I dedicate this book to my esteemed supervisors

Dr. Natwar Raj Kalla

Professor & Head, Dept of Biotechnology, MIET, Meerut; Professor (Retd.) & Ex-Chairman, Dept of Biophysics, Panjab University, Chandigarh; Former Secretary of Asian Society of Andrology

and

Dr. Pawan Kumar Mittal

Professor (Retd.), Dept of Zoology, Panjab University, Chandigarh

लक्ष्मी कान्ता चावला

दूरभाष : 0172-2740724 (कार्यालय)
0172-2747210 (कार्यालय)

अ० स० पत्र० क० . . . .

स्वास्थ्य एवं परिवार कल्याण मन्त्री,
पंजाब, चण्डीगढ़।

दिनांक 21-4-09

Sex, reproduction, contraception, family planning, sex education, etc. are the words that are looked down upon by conservative Indian society. Any discussion on these evokes a negative response from most of the people. Adolescents are unable to clarify their sex-related queries with the result that they get half-cooked or poorly-cooked knowledge from their peers which most of the times is not only inadequate but harmful for them. In the absence of adequate counseling facilities even the married couples are unable to get appropriate information on methods of contraception and spacing between children. Due to lack of knowledge, poor sexual hygiene and practices people suffer from so many sex-related problems and diseases. However, due to social stigma attached to these they do not seek medical advice.

This book written by Dr. Kuldeep Kaushik, Ph.D., is an effort in the right direction. The writer has taken a great initiative in writing this book that will be of great help to the millions of Indians, who are unable to get proper advice on sex and sex-related conditions due to various reasons.

The first part of the book deals with introduction to male and female reproductive systems, conception and child birth. This elementary knowledge will be helpful for everyone.

In the second and third parts various methods of contraception, i.e. birth control, their correct use, effect, advantages and disadvantages and even misconceptions have been discussed. National Family Welfare Programme and the benefits provided to the acceptors have been discussed in detail.

The fourth and last part outlines sex-related problems like masturbation, night emissions, sexual disorders and problems related to sexual activity.

From a common man's perspective this book is an excellent treatise on reproduction, contraception and sex written in simple and easily understandable language without the jargon of medical terminology.

Laxmi Kanta Chawla (Prof.)

Acknowledgements

I acknowledge myself for the entire work from initiation, authoring to compilation of this manuscript. I was inspired to create something informative, innovative and fruitful in my life that directed me towards writing a book which can highlight problems related to basic issues of marital and sexual life and offer proper guidance regarding those issues. I started working on it; shared views with my friends and colleagues and sought the opinions of public at large for a better creation. For all this, I pay my sincere regard to Landmark Education for providing me vital strength to complete this book.

I feel indebted to Dr. Manavjit Dhillon, CS Officer, (Ex-Medical Officer, Centre for Genetic Disorders, GNDU, Amritsar), for his valuable advice offered generously from time to time and for editing the manuscript.

I extend my thanks to Mr. Manish Sharma of Bharat Medical Store, Sri Ganganagar, Rajasthan for helping me to initiate this project and keeping my morale high. I am really grateful to him.

Dr. Subhash Chander Gangar, Dr. Ashok Bharti, Dr. Amit Sehgal, Dr. Rishi Tiwari (Patanjali Yogapeeth, Haridwar), Dr. Hardeep Mallh, Er. Kuljit Singh Takkar, Amandeep Walia, Amrit Kaur Bhullar, Talwinder Singh and Subhash Sharma (Amritsar) deserve sincere and heartfelt acknowledgments for their constant motivations and critical suggestions.

I may humbly say that this is an attempt to realize the dreams of my mother (Dr. Dulari Kaushik), father (Dr. Inder Parkash Kaushik), brother (Er. Naveen Kaushik) and the lovable and respectable people of my village, Romana Albel Singh, Faridkot, Punjab, India.

I also feel indebted to my beloved wife Advocate Sanju Sharma (Sanjana Kaushik) and my son Dev Veerum Pratap Kaushik (Chaitanya) for their patient love, unabated motivation as well as the support they provided throughout the gestation period of the book.

Kuldeep Kaushik

Contents

Introduction

This book is essentially an attempt to make the young Indians aware of certain facts related to reproduction, contraception, family planning and sex. This comprehensive book not only provides information in these fields but also emphasizes their interrelationships. A limited knowledge or lack of it, concerning the reproduction, contraception, family planning and sex can have a significant impact upon the social, family and personal life as well as growth and development of an individual.

Reading and seeing the pornographic material may enhance one's interest and thrust regarding sex but it seldom improves one's knowledge and skills in this field. Due to lack of knowledge of family planning and sex clinics in our areas/cities and certain myths prevailing in our modern society, sometimes awkward situations develop. This is now realized by both the partners that sex is not only meant for procreation but it is also a way of ultimate enjoyment and satisfaction and emotional and personal bonding. Safe sex and family planning without affecting individual health adds to the happy marital and sexual life.

The reproduction is a major issue in everyone's life, but unfortunately our society does not permit open discussion on it. It is believed that after marriage everyone has sufficient knowledge about it and can live without much problems related to reproduction. Certainly, modern society is highly educated and aware regarding reproduction but certain issues remain hidden throughout people's life.

Contraception plays a very significant role in the life of every committed couple. These days everyone knows about certain methods of contraception, but a limited knowledge about these few methods (i.e. contraceptive pills, emergency pills and condoms) is not sufficient for proper family planning. Family planning is usually visualized by people only as a method of safe sex. Family planning is the planning by the couples to maintain their healthy and happy marital and family life. No doubt, adopting the methods of family planning is very important for everyone and getting the knowledge of family planning is a greater issue rather than adopting the methods of family planning.

With the advancement in Indian society, everyone is more career conscious and due to this people are delaying their marriages and having children; hence, the practice of contraception assumes even greater significance. Contraception is effective when one has the knowledge of various forms of contraceptives and their application. Of course we are aware of the action mechanism of various contraceptives but this is really a worrying factor for us that most of us do not know how we can use these various types of contraceptives. We are also not sure about the various types of contraceptives, which are presently available in the Indian markets. Interestingly, only 50 per cent of married women are using contraceptives and other methods of family planning and out of this 85 per cent women rely on sterilization. Around 15 per cent women have unmet need of contraception for spacing as well as limiting the birth of child.

Another aspect is that, about 70 per cent of our total population lives in rural areas, which vary greatly in terms of economic, social, and religious lifestyles. It is observed that due to lack of proper knowledge and hesitation to consult about the various available methods, their family planning strategy totally depends upon contraceptive pills, condoms (provided by various family planning agencies) and on voluntary sterilization (government hospitals). It was also observed that in rural areas the national family planning programme is unable to reach the entire population effectively. In our nation, roughly 50 per cent of the population uses some form of birth control measures. I attended The Annual Congress of the Society of Andrology (SAI), India, jointly organized by IIT Kharagpur, NIHFW, New Delhi and SAI, India at NIHFW, New Delhi, from December 15-16, 2007, and I found that policymakers also pay more attention to sterilization techniques to avoid any further pregnancy risks. There is little emphasis on other temporary methods of family planning.

Now I am talking of a very serious, secret and touchy issue of life—sex. Sex problems are the burning issues in several families and may be a dominant cause of separation or divorce. If we look systematically and carefully at this, we can find out the way to get rid of these problems.

The book *Human Reproduction, Contraception, Family Planning and Sex* covers all the queries and problems of the individual pertaining to reproduction, contraception, family planning and sex and provides effective and practical answers. It has been broadly divided under following four topics:

- Reproduction
- Contraception
- Family Planning
- Sex and Sex Problems

The reproduction section deals with the basics of reproduction, including anatomy (structure and function) of reproductive organs, sex hormones, menstruation cycle and semen analysis—directly associated with contraception and fertility. The book also provides information regarding some physiological changes that occur after conception, sequential development changes in fetus and some information about childbirth.

The contraception section covers all the modern methods of contraception which are available in Indian markets. The advantages, disadvantages, action mechanisms and side effects of the condoms, pills, IUD, spermicidal agents, emergency pills, MT pills and abortion are elaborately discussed in the relevant chapters. I have also tried to enlist all the branded contraceptives which are easily available in Indian markets.

There are certain permanent methods of family planning like tubectomy and vasectomy which are highly effective. The affects of prevailing myths are more dominant over the few actual side effects of these methods. This section deals with the myths associated with various contraceptive methods. The section also throws light on government policy of family planning, financial help provided by it including the financial assistance offered during any mishappening caused by the failure of these methods.

The last section of the book studies the highly delicate issue of life—sex. It can help you to diagnose certain problems related to sex and the factors (medical or psychological) associated with them. It will also help you whenever you or your partner faces any kind of problem.

Kuldeep Kaushik

Reproduction

1. Female: Reproductive System
2. Menstruation Cycle and Fertility
3. Female Sex Hormones
4. Male: Reproductive System and Sex Hormones
5. Semen
6. Conception and Childbirth

1

Female: Reproductive System

In sexual reproduction two types of sex i.e. male and female participate for the production of the progeny. For the better understanding of reproduction and contraception, the basic knowledge of the reproductive system of both the sexes is essential for everyone.

Female Reproductive System

Female reproductive system is specifically designed to produce ova, fertilization, transportation and implantation into the uterus as well as sexual intercourse. Reproductive system of female is located entirely in the pelvis (that's the lowest part of the abdomen).

Female reproductive system contains

- External genitalia
- Internal reproductive system

1. External Genitalia

These are the external part of female reproductive organs which are characteristic feminine features. These play an important role in the sexual stimulation or arousing the sexuality.

Vulva: The external part of the female reproductive organs is called the vulva, which covers the opening to the vagina as well as other reproductive organs located inside the body. The vulva is the proper word for the entire area between a girl or woman's legs.

Hymen: This is a thin sheet of tissue or a membrane that covers the opening of the vagina. Hymen also contains one or more holes for the proper flow of the menses. It is observed that during first sexual intercourse it is stretched or torn and some bleeding may occur with little, if any, pain. Some women who already had sex don't have much of a change in their hymen, though. Hymen is usually not observed in players and actively working woman.

Clitoris: This is a small sensory organ, is located toward the front of the vulva where the folds of the labia join. It is a very important part for the experience of sexual arousal in girls and women but it may be hard to find because it is hooded with skin.

Mons Pubis: At the top of the vaginal opening as well the clitoris, the fleshy area covered with pubic hair in the sexually matured females is called mons pubis.

Labia Minora: The vaginal opening surrounded by two flaps like skin folds from both sides is called labia minora. The labia minora does not have fat or padding. Instead it has blood vessels, oil glands, and scent glands.

Labia Majora: These are fleshy pair of the lips surrounding the labia minora and are found below the mons pubis. Like mons pubis these are also covered by the pubic hair in sexually mature girls.

Between the labia are openings to the urethra (the canal that carries urine from the bladder to the outside of the body) and vagina.

2. Internal Reproductive System

Main function of the internal reproductive system is the production of viable ova, its fertilization, transportation, implantation into uterus as well as supporting the growth of developing fetus. But these events takes place only after the sexual copulation or intercourse, which is the most essential act for the deposition of sperms, fertilization and the development of fetus. A female's internal reproductive organs are the vagina, uterus, fallopian tubes, and ovaries.

Vagina: This is 3 to 5 inches long muscular, hollow tube that extends from the vaginal opening to the uterus. The vagina's muscular walls are lined with mucous membranes, which keep it protected and moist. During sexual intercourse, it accommodates male organ (penis) and semen is deposited from male partner at the sexual climax.

Contraction and expansion is the unique property of vagina (due to muscular walls) which helps in sexual intercourse, sperm transportation as well as provides the pathways during the childbirth. Secondly, this is the only route for the menstrual blood (the period) to leave the body from the uterus.

Uterus (Womb): The uterus is a pear shaped hollow, thick-walled muscular organ located in the female pelvis above the vagina. Uterus is attached with vagina through the cervix. This is the lower narrow portion of the uterus and it protrudes downward into the opening of the vaginal canal. During childbirth, the cervix can expand to allow a baby to pass. From the lateral side, it is attached with ovary through the fallopian or uterine tubes which act as a channel for eggs from the ovary to travel to the uterus.

The main function of the uterus is to nourish the developing fetus prior to birth. During pregnancy the uterus expands to accommodate a developing embryo. Once the egg has left the ovary it can be fertilized and it implants itself in the thickened lining of the uterus. If an egg is not fertilized, the thickened uterine lining sloughs off in a process known as menstruation bleeding.

Fallopian Tubes: These are about 4 inches long tubes attached to the sides of uterus and have a very tiny passageway no wider than a sewing needle. Blockages of these tubes are the major casual factor of the female infertility.

Fallopian tube has a funnel like fringe area at the other end that wraps around the ovary but doesn't completely attach to it. When an egg pops out of an ovary, it enters the fallopian tube. Once the egg is in the fallopian tube, tiny hairs in the tube's lining help push it in the narrow passageway towards the uterus.

Ovary: It is the part inside the female body where ova or eggs are produced. These are two oval-shaped organs that lie to the upper right and left of the uterus. Ovaries release single egg alternatively every month at the 14th day of menstruation cycle, this process is known as ovulation.

Besides the production of viable eggs these are the main source of female hormones (estrogen and progesterone). These hormones control the development of female body characteristics, such as the breasts, body shape, and body hair. The ovaries also regulate the menstrual cycle and pregnancy.

2

Menstruation Cycle And Fertility

Menstrual Cycle (MC)

Menstruation is the shedding of the inner lining of womb along with bleeding through a woman's vagina. Menstruation is also called monthly bleeding, menstrual course, menses, menstrual period and period. This process occurs once a month during a woman's reproductive age. It is commonly known as monthly blood-flow through the vagina in which the endometrium is completely shed-down by the uterus at the end of its reproductive cycle. The menstrual cycle is a recurring cycle of physiologic changes that occurs in reproductive-age of females. The average age of starting the menstruation in humans is 11-13 years, but some factors such as heredity, diet and overall health can accelerate or delay its onset. A woman's first menstruation is termed as menarche, and is one of the initial stages of puberty in girls. The cessation of menstrual cycles at the end of a woman's reproductive life is termed as menopause. The average age of menopause in women is 51 years, with a range anywhere between 40 and 58 years.

Some important Points about MC:

- The average length of menstrual cycle is around 28 days.
- Normally, regular menstruation lasts for 3 to 5 days, but can be anywhere between 2 to 7 days which is considered normal.
- The flow of menses normally serves as a sign that a woman has not become pregnant, after an unprotected sex.
- During the reproductive years, failure to menstruate may provide the first indication to a woman that she may have become pregnant.
- During menstruation, blood is also lost along with the shedding of the endometrial tissue and the average blood loss is 35 milliliters with a range of 10–80 ml considered normal.

Some Disorders of MC (Problems)

Dysmenorrhea: This is the most common menstruation problem. This is a painful menstruation (usually severe cramp in the lower abdominal parts). Some women uses certain pain killers to overcome this problem.

Menorrhagia or Hypermenorrhea: It is the abnormal menses flow in which women have heavy and sudden flows with amounts in excess of 80 ml.

Hypomenorrhea: In which women have a very little flow (less than 10 ml).

Polymenorrhea: Is the condition in which length of the menses is reduced and women frequently undergo these cycles and it is the medical term for the cycles with intervals of 21 days or less.

Oligomenorrhea: Is the condition in which duration of the cycle exceeds to 35 days repeatedly.

Amenorrhea: It refers to a prolonged absence of menses during the reproductive years of a woman and intervals of cycle exceed 180 days. This condition is frequently observed in the athletes having very little body fat.

Primary Amenorrhea: When the woman has never had cycle before.

Secondary Amenorrhea: When the woman earlier had cycles/periods, but later they stopped.

Prolonged flow (metrorrhagia, also meno-metrorrhagia) no longer shows a clear interval pattern. Dysfunctional uterine bleeding refers to hormonally caused flow abnormalities, typically anovulation.

All bleeding problems as well menstrual abnormalities need medical attention; as they may indicate hormone imbalances, uterine fibroids, or some other reasons. As pregnant patient may also bleed so a pregnancy test forms a part of the evaluation of the abnormal flow.

Fundamentals of Menstrual Cycle

Starting of the flow of the menses or bleeding is counted as the first day of the menstrual cycle. This cycle may be divided into several phases on the basis of endometrium or follicle development and the length of each phase varies from woman to woman and cycle to cycle. Average values are shown below:

On the Basis of Follicle Changes

Sl. No.	Name of phase	Days
1.	Menstrual Phase	1–4
2.	Follicular Phase	5–13
3.	Ovulation	14
4.	Luteal Phase	15–28

On the Basis of Endometrial Changes

Sl. No.	Name of Phase	Days
1.	Menstrual Phase	1–4
2.	Proliferative Phase	5–13
3.	Ovulation	14
4.	Secretory Phase	15–28

Many women experience uterine cramps during this time (severe cramps or other symptoms are called dysmenorrhea), as well as other **premenstrual syndrome** symptoms. A vast industry of sanitary products has grown to help women during their menstruation. During the reproductive years, failure to menstruate may provide the first indication to a woman that she may have become pregnant. (However, this cannot be taken as certainty, as sometimes there is some flow of blood in early pregnancy.)

Phases of the Menstrual Cycle

1. Menstrual Phase

It is the initial phase **of menstrual bleeding** and also indicates that a woman has not become pregnant. Normal and regular menstruation usually takes 3 to 5 days. Normally menstruating woman loose around 10–80 ml blood in each cycles but due to some physiological factors the amount of blood lost may increase. Due to this large blood loss, women have higher dietary requirements for iron than the males to prevent iron deficiency.

2. Follicular Phase/Proliferative Phase

This is the phase of the follicular development and the follicles which is the progenitor of functional ovum. Ovary contains large number of follicles but under the influence of certain hormones only one goes in to the functional state. Under the influence of a rise in follicle stimulating hormone (FSH), five to seven tertiary-stage ovarian follicles are recruited for entry into the next menstrual cycle. All but one of these follicles will undergo *atresia*, while one (or occasionally two) dominant follicles will progress to maturity. As they mature, the follicles secrete increasing amounts of estradiol, an estrogen.

The estrogens that follicles secrete initiate the formation of a new layer of endometrium in the uterus, histologically identified as the proliferative endometrium. The estrogen also stimulates crypts in the cervix to produce fertile cervical mucus, which may be noticed by women practicing fertility awareness.

3. Ovulation

Ultimate goal of female reproductive system is to produce the ova for production of new generation. It usually occurs at the 14th day of normal menstruating cycle. When the egg has matured, it secretes enough estradiol to trigger the acute release of luteinizing hormone (LH). In the average cycle this LH surge starts around day 12th of the cycle and may last for 48 hours. The release of LH matures the egg and weakens the wall of the follicle in the ovary. This process leads to ovulation: the release of the now matured ovum. The egg is swept into the fallopian tube by the fimbria—a finger like structure at the end of each fallopian tube.

It was also observed that few women feel characteristic abdominal pain at the time of ovulation which may last a few hours. Light mid-cycle blood flow from the vagina of some women is also observed due to the sudden change in hormones at the time of ovulation

4. Luteal Phase/Secretory Phase

After releasing the viable ova (ovum) residual follicle get converted into the corpus luteum, a solid body formed in the ovaries under the influence of the pituitary hormones. This corpus luteum will produce progesterone in addition to estrogens for approximately the next two weeks.

Progesterone plays a vital role in converting the proliferative endometrium into a secretory lining receptive for implantation and supportive of the early pregnancy. It slightly raises the body temperature; hence women who record their basal body temperature on a daily basis will notice that they have entered the luteal phase.

After fertilization, egg is converted into an early blastocyst in the fallopian tube and migrates to the uterus for the implantation after 6 to 12 days of ovulation. Shortly after implantation, the growing embryo will signal its existence to the maternal system. This signal has an important role in maintaining the corpus luteum and enabling it to continue to produce progesterone. One very early signal consists of human chorionic gonadotropin (hCG), a hormone that pregnancy tests can measure.

In the absence of a pregnancy and without hCG, the corpus luteum demises and inhibin and progesterone levels fall. This will set the stage for the next cycle. Progesterone withdrawal leads to menstrual shedding (*progesterone withdrawal bleeding*), and falling inhibin levels allow FSH levels to rise to raise a new crop of follicles.

KEY FACTS OF MC

1. Menstrual phase is the very first phase i.e. bleeding phase.
2. During the follicular phase the lining of the uterus thickens, stimulated by gradually increasing amounts of estrogen.
3. Follicles in the ovary begin developing under the influence of a complex interplay of hormones, and after several days one or occasionally two follicles become dominant (non-dominant follicles atrophy and die).
4. The dominant follicle releases an ovum or egg in an event called ovulation.
5. After ovulation egg is transported through the fallopian tube where the fertilization takes place.
6. Fertilized egg usually takes one to two weeks to travels in the fallopian tubes and then it reaches the uterus.
7. After ovulation the remains of the dominant follicle in the ovary becomes corpus luteum; this body has a primary function of producing large amounts of progesterone.
8. Under the influence of progesterone, the endometrium (uterine lining) undergoes changes to prepare for the potential implantation of an embryo to establish the pregnancy.
9. If the egg is not fertilized within a day of ovulation, it will die and will be shed in the menstrual bleeding.
10. If implantation does not occur within approximately two weeks, the corpus luteum will die, causing sharp drops in levels of both

progesterone and estrogen. These hormone drops cause the uterus to shed its lining in a process termed as menstruation.

Fertile Periods and Fertile Window

Women should be advised that the timing of their fertile window could be highly unpredictable, even if their cycles are usually regular. This is a highly rough estimation if we consider the same for safe sexual intercourse. To avoid an unwanted pregnancy following fact should be kept in mind:

1. Life span of viable spermatozoa inside a woman's reproductive system ranges from 1-5 days
2. Ovulation usually takes place at 14th day after the beginning of the menses, if menstrual cycles are around 28 days and regular. But this is not always true and this assumption may lead to unintended pregnancies.
3. It is observed (from the scientific data) that the length of the follicular phase and consequently the length of the menstrual cycle may vary from person to person, widely.
4. If a woman wants to conceive, the most fertile time occurs between 8 and 18 days from the first day of the menses.
5. Female generally detects their ovulation on the basis of following one or more of the three primary fertility signs i.e. basal body temperature, cervical fluid, and cervical position.

3

Female Sex Hormones

These are the specific hormones which determine the feminine characteristics and are also responsible for the development of the secondary sexual organs, menstruation cycle as well as the maintenance of the pregnancy. Sex hormones are primarily secreted by the ovarian tissue but placenta and adrenal glands also takes part. Besides the female sex hormones, ovary also secretes some of the male hormones like testosterone (which is also essential for the proper growth of the female). Females have mainly following sex hormones which determines the different functions in the body:

Gonadal Hormones

1. Estrogen
2. Progesterone
3. Testosterone

Pituitary and Hypothalamic Hormones

4. Follicular stimulating hormone (FSH)
5. Luteinizing hormone (LH)

Placental Hormones

6. Human chorionic gonadotropin (hCG)

1. Estrogen

This is the main sex hormone in the female secreted by ovary and it governs the following functions in the pubertal stage:

- Stimulates breast development.
- Stimulates the development and maturation of vagina, uterus (womb) and Fallopian tubes (that carry eggs to the womb) to mature.
- Development of other faminine characteristics like, softness in voice, emotions, shyness and physical absence of hair on facial and other body part like chest, legs, arms, etc.
- Specific deposition of fat around very specific areas of hips, buttocks and thighs.
- Role in ovulation and pregnancy.
- Role in bone density modulation (male + female).
- Role in mineral, carbohydrate, protein and lipid metabolism.

2. Progesterone

This is produced by corpus luteum in the ovary and hence called luteal hormone. It also performs the following tasks in the female body:

- Responsible for menstruation.
- Maintain the pregnancy.
- Prevention of spontaneous uterine contractions.
- Inhibition of follicular maturation and ovulation and hence remains virtually absent prior to ovulation.
- Development of endometrium.
- Promotes development of the tubules and alveoli of the breasts, causing the alveolar cells to proliferate, enlarge, and become secretory in nature but not to secrete milk.

3. Testosterone

In the female reproductive system this hormone is secreted by the theca cells of Graffian follicles (one layer of cells of Graffian follicles).

- Testosterone helps to promote muscle and bone growth.
- It stimulates sexual desire and is also called the libido hormone.

4. Follicular Stimulating Hormone (FSH)

Follicle stimulating hormone (FSH) is a hormone synthesized and secreted by gonadotropes in the anterior pituitary gland and act synergistically with LH in reproduction. it is known for the following functions:

- Stimulates the development of egg (stimulate immature Graafian follicles toward maturation).
- Administration of FSH to humans and animals induces "superovulation", or development of more than the usual number of mature follicles and hence, an increased number of mature gametes.
- FSH testing is commonly used to evaluate a:
  - I. Woman's egg supply (ovarian reserve).
  - II. Help evaluate menstrual problems, such as irregular or absent menstrual periods (amenorrhea).

5. Luteinizing Hormone (LH)

Along with the FSH, this is also synthesised and secreted by gonadotropes in the anterior pituitary gland. The principal functions of LH are:

1. Promoting the androgen synthesis in the thecal cells of the ovaries.
2. Inducing ovulation (by stimulating the cascade of proteolytic enzymes leading to the rupture of the basement membrane of the follicle) and
3. Maintaining the corpus luteum during the menstrual cycle.

1. Ovulation of mature follicles on the ovary is induced by a large burst of LH secretion known as the preovulatory LH surge.

6. Human Chorionic Gonadotropin (hCG)

This is marker hormone of pregnancy, which is usually detected in the urine after one week of conception. Suspected pregnant woman can confirm their pregnancy by urine test (Strips, easily available in the market). This is produced by the placenta of the pregnant woman.

- It maintain the viablity of the corpus luteum in the ovary and thereby maintain progesterone production that is critical for a pregnancy in humans
- Multiple pregnancy can also be determined by the quantitative estimation of hCG.

All above mentioned female Sex hormone are responsible for the development of female, feminine characteristics, production of egg and their successful fertilization and prenatal development as well as nourishment of fetus.

Hormonal Significance, Synthesis and Their Interplay

At certain age of girl's life, breasts will get bigger, underarm, pubic hair will develop, body pattern will change, emotional turbulence will occur, the onset of fertility and sexuality will emerge.

These characteristics are not a random but a systematic process and strictly controlled by hormones. Few girls experience difficulties in adapting to their changing body pattern due to the changes in the hormonal patterns at the age of puberty.

Not only these pubertal characteristics but maintenance of menstruation, pregnancy, development of baby, production as well as secretion of milk is tightly controlled by the sex hormones. It has been observed that these hormones are significantly related and influence the role of each other.

Each individual hormone (LH, FSH, estrogen and progesterone) follows its own pattern, rising and falling at different points in the cycle but together they produce a predictable chain of events, all playing a vital role in regulating a woman's menstrual cycle, which results in her periods. Ovary contains several hundred immature eggs but in every cycle one egg becomes 'ripe' (mature) and is released. Graffian follicle converts to corpus luteum and ovum starts to move in the fallopian tube and into the womb. If that egg is not fertilized the ovary plans the formation of a new viable egg and the levels of estrogen and progesterone produced by the ovary begin to fall which also supports the development of the womb. Without the supporting action of these hormones, the lining of the womb, which is full of blood, is shed, resulting in a period.

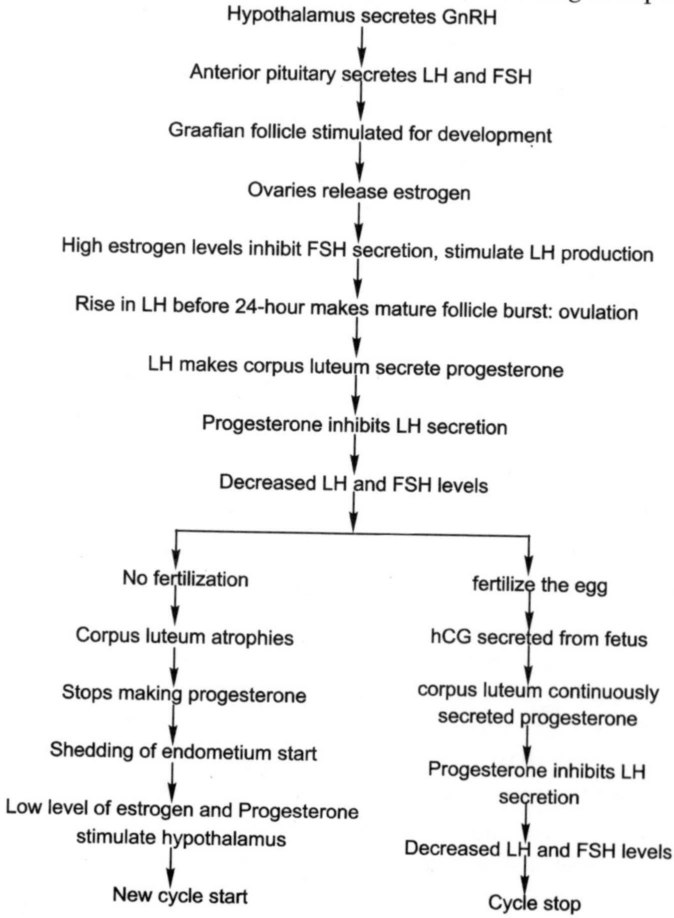

Decrease the level of estrogen and progesterone in the blood stimulate hypothalamus (part of brain) which secrete GnRH. The GnRH stimulates pituitary gland in brain (also called master gland) to secrete LH and FSH and new menstrual cycle start.

Hormone and Contraception (Menstruation Options)

Hormones not only control female physiology but also have a significant role in the contraception. Normally contraceptives contain estrogens and progesterone or their analogues or their derivatives, which have a significant effect on menstruation cycle as well as on fertility of the females.

Contraceptive Pills

These contain estrogens and progesterone (combined pills) and/or progesterone alone (Mini pills). They do not obstruct the regular monthly flow but suppress ovulation (progesterone block the LH surge). Monthly pills contained in pack of 28 pills (for 28 days, each daily) in which a woman takes hormone pills for 21 days, followed by 7 days of non-functional placebo pills/iron pills.

After day 21 supply of hormone is blocked, which initiate menses flow. If woman skips the placebos and continue with the next batch of hormone pills without interval, it may suppress monthly bleeding up to next cycle. It is useful method as for some religious purpose women can avoid monthly bleeding. Monthly bleeding at certain precious time like wedding night, anniversary time or certain other occasion is really unwanted, one can avoid this situation by using these pills.

4

Male: Reproductive System and Sex Hormones

Male reproductive system is specifically designed to produce sperm, sex hormones as well as proper transfer of sperms (ejaculation) into the female reproductive system for successful fertilization. The male reproductive system contains external genitalia and internal duct system of vas deferens, seminal vesicle and accessory glands. In general male reproductive system contains:

External Genitalia:

- Penis
- Testis

Duct System:

- Epididymis
- Vas Deferens

Accessory Glands:

- Seminal Vesicles
- Accessory Glands

1. The Penis

The penis is the copulatory organ of the males and has a long shaft and enlarged tip called the glans penis. At the end of the glans is a small slit or opening, which is where semen and urine exit the body through the urethra. When the male is sexually aroused, the penis becomes hard, erect and ready for intercourse.

The male penis is made of two different tissues, soft spongy tissue and cartilage. The inside of the penis is made of a spongy tissue that can expand and contract. Erection is achieved because blood sinuses within the erectile tissue of the penis become filled with blood. The arteries of the penis are dilated while the veins are passively compressed so that blood flows into the erectile cartilage under pressure.

2. The Testis

These are the main parts of the male reproductive system and they hang out in the scrotal pouch just below the penis. The scrotal pouch contains two oval shape testicles. There are two major functions of testes i.e.:

- Sperm production
- Testosterone secretion (male sex hormone)

Testis is always found in the scrotal sacs outside the body cavity which provide slightly cooler environment. This environment is necessary for the proper production of the sperm. Increase in the testicles temperature or movement into abdomen leads to infertility due to blockage of sperm production. This condition frequently observed in few new born children is called "Cryptorchidism". Testis produces millions of sperms per day.

Testosterone is the main sex hormone and is responsible for puberty in boys i.e. development of stronger muscles, body and facial hair, deeper voice, aggressiveness and it also stimulates the production of sperms.

3. The Epididymis

It is a structure within the scrotum in the form of a long coiled tube around 18-20 feet in length, attached to the backside of the testis. The epididymis is a coiled segment of the spermatic ducts that serves to store, mature and transport spermatozoa between the testis and the vas deferens.

It receives sperms from the rete testis (part of testis) and handover them to the vas deferens. During their transit in the epididymis, sperms undergo maturation processes necessary for them to acquire fertlization functions. It prevents the earlier capacitation, the final maturation process which is completed in the female reproductive tract.

4. The Vas Deferens

The vas deferens is a muscular tube that passes upward alongside the testicles and transports the sperm-containing fluid called **semen**. At the end of this tubular structure, there is an ampulla (expanded tube).

5. Ejaculatory Duct

The urethra is the channel that carries the semen to the outside of the body through the penis. The urethra is also part of the urinary system because it is also the channel through which urine passes as it leaves the urinary bladder and exits the body. Urethra - conducts urine and sperm.

6. The Accessory Glands

A. The Seminal Vesicles

Seminal vesicle is a pouch like pair of glands situated on each side of the male urinary bladder that secrete seminal fluid and nourishes and promotes the movement of spermatozoa through the urethra. Semen is the main secretion of the seminal vesicles which contains proteins, fructose sugar, vitamin C, enzymes phosphorylcholine and prostaglandins.

Prostaglandins secreted by the seminal vesicles perform several functions. It helps in the motility of sperms as well as their capacitation (necessary for fertilization) and cause reverse peristalsis in uterus and uterine tubes, decrease mucus viscosity at cervix. Thus it makes the fertilization process easier.

B. The Prostate Gland

Prostatic fluid which is slightly alkaline in nature is the second major contributor in the formation of semen. Prostate surrounds the ejaculatory ducts at the base of the **urethra** just below the bladder. The alkalinity of the seminal fluid helps to neutralize the acidity of the vaginal tract, thus prolonging the lifespan of sperm.

Prostate also contains some proteolytic enzymes that liquefy coagulated semen after 15-20 minutes in vagina and seminal plasmin that have certain antibiotic properties which destroys bacteria present in the semen.

C. The Bulbourethral Gland

Bulbourethral glands are found at the base of the penis, in the deep of the perineal pouch. The glands almost equals to the size of a pea.

At the time of the sexual excitement or foreplay, one or two drops of a clear viscous secretion come out from the penis, and are called pre-ejaculate, is the secretion of this gland. It secretes alkaline mucoids, a fluid which helps to lubricate the urethra for the spermatozoa to pass through, it neutralizes traces of acidic urine in the urethra. It clears the urinic environment as well as foreign particles present in the urethra.

Male Sex Hormones

Production and releasing the semen into female reproductive system during sexual intercourse is the ultimate goal and role of male sex hormones.

During early part of the development of a fetus/child, except the genetalia, the body of the boys and girls is almost similar. Reproductive system is also in an immature stage and unable to reproduce. It is only the sex hormones that differentiates the sexes and makes them reproductive and fertile. Males produce testosterone which is responsible for masculinity in the individual.

During early puberty (10 to 14 years) the pituitary gland, which is located near the brain secretes hormones that stimulates the testicles to produce testosterone. The production of testosterone brings about many physical changes. Although the timing of these changes is different for every person, the stages of puberty generally follows a set sequence of events.

1. The scrotum and testes grow larger.
2. Penis becomes longer, and the seminal vesicles and prostate gland grows.
3. Hairs begin to appear in the pubic area and later it grows on the face and the underarms.

During the mean time males become muscular and attain their specific height/weight, voice changes, aggressiveness and develop masculinity and the formation of the sperms starts.

Common problems of Male Reproductive System

Hypospadias: This is the major disorder of the penis in which the urethra opens on the underside of the penis and not at the tip (glans). Due to this male cannot deposit their semen properly into the vagina. The length of penis is also affected by hypospadias.

Plastic or micro surgery is recommended for these patients during early childhood to correct this condition.

Inflammation of the Penis: itching, swelling, redness and pain are the few symptoms of penile inflammation.

- Balanitis occurs when the glans (the head of the penis) becomes inflamed. It usually causes redness and/or blotchy rashes on the glans, itching and discomfort, sometimes accompanied with a discharge. This can be avoided by proper cleaning and drying glans as well as the foreskin. One common organism associated with balanitis is yeast (fungus) known as *Candida albicans*.
- Posthitis is the foreskin or prepuce inflammation, which is usually due to a yeast or bacterial infection.

Varicocele: Blood enters into the testis through arteries and drain out through veins. In testis, varicose vein performs blood drainage function. Upward flow of blood in the veins is ensured by small one-way valves that prevent backflow. Defective valves, or compression of the vein by a nearby structure, can cause dilatation of the veins near the testis, leading to the formation of a varicocele. It can be observed by feeling of palpable veins or the heaviness in the testicles, dragging and aching pain in the scrotum. Prolonged condition of varicocele leads to infertility.

Hydrocele: A condition in which serous fluids accumulates, in the membranes surrounding the testis. In some cases, surgery may be needed to correct the condition. Hydroceles are common in newborn infants. During normal development, the testicles descend down via a tube from the abdomen into the scrotum. Hydroceles result when this tube fails to close. Fluid drains from the abdomen through the open tube into the scrotum. Hydrocele may cause swelling in the scrotum around the testicles but is generally painless.

Inguinal Hernia: Testis migrates to the scrotal sac during development through inguinal canal which is then reduced. Hernia is the condition in which there is protrusion of the abdominal cavity contents through the inguinal canal making their way into the scrotum. When a portion of the intestines pushes through an abnormal opening or the weakening of the abdominal wall and into the groin or scrotum, it is known as the inguinal hernia.

5

Semen

During sexual intercourse and/or ejaculation, sperms are released from the penis in specific fluid called semen. Semen is the thick, white, sperm-containing fluid released during ejaculation.

Semen contains germ cells (sperm) and seminal fluid or seminal plasma. Seminal fluid is the mixture of sugar, protein, zinc, proteins and certain other components secreted by various glands associated with the male reproductive system. Each component of the seminal fluid has a particular function. Seminal fluid is basic in nature and it stimulates and provides the energy for the sperm movement as well as its active gradient initiates the contractions in the uterine cavity for the movement of sperm. Evaluation of certain parameters of sperm as well as the seminal fluid (seminal plasma) determines the quality of semen.

Semen Analysis

Analysis of the semen is one of the most essential tests for the couples consulting for the conception as well as for the evaluation of the male infertility. It is a relatively simple and inexpensive clinical test but should be performed in an andrology, IVF lab where a high volume of semen studies is done. Semen analysis includes the examination of:

- Seminal fluid
- Spermatozoa
- Other cells present in semen

Before analysis of semen sample following points should be followed carefully:

- Period of sexual abstinence (3-5 days)
- Complete sampling
- Timing of sampling
- Appearance of semen (color, viscosity and abnormal smell)
- Duration of liquefaction. If it takes more than 60 minutes, treat the sample with bromelin for further biophysical and biochemical tests.

A Few Basic Biophysical Estimations

Sl. No.	Standard Tests	Normal Values
1.	Volume	2.0 ml or more
2.	pH	7.2-7.8
3.	Sperm concentration	20 x 106 spermatozoa/ml or more
4.	Total sperm count	40 x 106 spermatozoa or more
5.	Vitality	75% or more live
6.	Motility	50% or more with forward progression or 25% or more with rapid progression within 60 min after collection
7.	Morphology	30% or more with normal morphology
8.	White blood cells	Fewer than 1 x 106/ml

A Few Basic Biochemical Estimations

Sl. No.	Standard Tests	Normal Values
1.	Zinc (total)	2.4 mmole or more per ejaculate
2.	Citric acid (total)	52 mmole or more per ejaculate
3.	Fructose (total)	13 mmole or more per ejaculate
4.	Carnitine	0.8-2.9 mmole per ejaculate
5.	Acid phosphatase (total)	200 U or more per ejaculate
6.	a-glucosidase (neutral	20 mU or more per ejaculate

There are certain other specific sperm function tests which are not mentioned in this chapter which are done upon the suggestion of an Andrologist.

Sperm or Spermatozoa

This is the only cell present in the semen which is responsible for the actual fertilization of the ova and the subsequent development of the baby.

These are highly motile cells and travel a significant distance from vagina to fallopian tubes via cervix and uterus for fertilization. Fertilization or union of sperm and ova (egg) is the basis of propagation of life.

A mature sperm has 3 distinct parts: a head, a mid-piece, and a tail. Head carries the genetic material which determines the sex of child i.e. boy or girl or in other words, ***Man is responsible for the sex of child i.e. boy or girl.*** Male produces following two types of sperm:

1. Sperm containing (22+X) chromosomes
2. Sperm containing (22+Y) chromosomes

Fertilization with sperm containing "X" chromosomes produces a girl and with sperm containing "Y" produces a boy. ***Females produce only one type of egg and are not responsible for the determination of sex.***

Middle piece and tail provide the motility to sperms which is also a major factor responsible for fertility. A normal human male usually produces several hundred million sperms per day. Sperm are continuously produced throughout a male's reproductive life, though production decreases with age. There are certain following factors which are used in the analysis of fertile sperms:

- Sperm count (Numbers of sperm/ml)
- Shape of head
- Motility of sperm

Classification of the semen sample on the basis of sperm characters

Normozoospermia: When all the spermatozoal parameters as well as other parameters related to seminal plasma are normal.

Oligozoospermia: When sperm count is reduced as compared to the normal fertile man and it is counted to be less than 20 million/ml.

Teratozoospermia: When the shape of a sperm's head is not normal and less than 50 per cent of the spermatozoa with normal morphology are observed.

Asthenozoospermia: when the average sperm motility is find to be reduced. Fewer than 50 per cent spermatozoa with forward progression are observed.

Oligoasthenoteratozoospermia: Signifies disturbance of all the three variables i.e. count, movement and shape of the spermatozoa.

Azoospermia: No spermatozoa are observed in the ejaculate.

Aspermia: No ejaculate at all.

6

Conception and Childbirth

Conception

It is the process in which fertilized egg (blastocyst) attaches to the uterine wall. It occurs around 7-10 days after the unprotected sex, during fertile period (unsafe period i.e. 8-18 days from the menses). It is slow and a systematic process involving following steps:

1. **Intercourse**: It is required for fertilization, during this process the sperms are released from male partner into female's internal genitalia and millions of sperms move to the fallopian tube through the uterus.
2. **Fertilization**: Around 14th day of menses, single egg is automatically released from the ovary and is transported to the womb (uterus) through the fallopian tubes. Fertilization is the process in which **one sperm enters into the ovum** (egg) and makes a new cell (zygote), the basis of a new life. Some facts of fertilization:
   - It occurs in fallopian tube
   - It is a complex process which takes around 24 hours after penetration of sperms into the ova (egg).

- End product of fertilization is the "Zygote", the first cell of new baby.
- Zygote has characters of both parents.
- **Fertilized egg (zygote) has the potential to develop into a child** and starts multiplication for the development and growth of the fetus.
- Zygote converts into blastomere (2-8 cells), it takes around 20 hours for the first cell division and then into the morula (8-16 cells).
- The morula travels out of the fallopian tube and reaches the endometrial cavity (uterus or womb).

3. **Implantation:** In uterus morula converts into blastocyst, a plastic ball like structure. Implantation occurs approximately 7-10 days after fertilization, and it is initiated when the blastocyst comes into contact with the uterine wall.

   The outer layer of cells gives rise to the placenta, and other supporting tissues needed for fetal development within the uterus while the inner cell mass cells give rise to the tissues or organs of the baby. **Implantation is the first step of the pregnancy**

Early Signs and Symptoms of Pregnancy

There are some signs of implantation or successful conception in a pregnant woman, which may also be seen without any conception. These signs are just an indication, and therefore further confirmation is required by standard test and or examination.

Before relating these physiological changes or sign to pregnancy, attention should be paid on timing of intercourse (sex during fertile time or window). There are certain following early signs of pregnancy

- **Implantation bleeding or cramping:** Before the due date of next menses (from 20-24 days of menses) some women may experience implantation spotting, a slight staining of a pink or brown colour. Cramping is also observed along with spotting.

- **Morning sickness faces:** Few days after conception, some woman may begin feeling nauseated and uneasy. Pregnancy-related nausea is not strictly related to the morning time but can be observed anytime during morning, noon, or night.
- **Altered taste of mouth** (**Sense of taste**): It is frequently observed that taste of mouth is totally changed and some have permanently metallic taste through out their pregnancy and the taste of food they usually like i.e. coffee, tea, or others is also altered.
- **Food cravings or aversions:** During these days, funny little food cravings or aversions will appear. In Indian society woman usually start to takes pickles, also called "Khatta khana". During aversions, some women even avert by the smell or site of the food.
- Vomiting is also considered as a potent sign of pregnancy in Indian cultured.
- Increase in the tenderness of nipple and size of breasts.
- Feeling highly tired and fatigued during early pregnancy.
- Implantation changes the hormonal level which increases the frequency of urination.
- Skin around the nipples gets darker after successful conception, this may also be due to the effect of previous pregnancy or it may signal of a hormonal imbalance unrelated to pregnancy.

Conformational Pregnancy Tests

Menstruation delay along with above-mentioned symptoms can point towards the probability of conception in regularly menstruating women, yet further strip test is also recommended.

Pregnancy Test at Home

With this test woman can confirm her pregnancy within a week, after the due date of menses with the help of pregnancy test strips. These are easily available in the market.

For the test, collect the urine in a detergent free container and dip the strip up to a mark i.e. usually prescribed by the manufacturer. Appearance of the desired band confirms the pregnancy. Sometimes band may be faint; this could be due to low levels of hCG hormone and repeat the test with a new strip after
72 hours. In case no bands appear, then the test is invalid and again repeats the test after 72 hours with the new strip.

Further confirmation can be done with the help of sonography.

Highlights of Fetal Development
Specific feature of a child during the gestation periods

Age (Month)	Appearance of the fetus
1st	1. Fertilized egg is about the size of pigeon's egg 2. Length 1 cm and weight around 2.5 gm 3. Eyes are seen as 2 dark spots 4. Lenses appear as buds like processes 5. Heart begins development the third week and begins beating the 4th week
2nd	1. Length 4 cm and weight around 15 gm 2. Eyes and nose are recognizable 3. Anus is seen as dark spot 4. Umbilical cord begins to develop 5. Arms and legs formed 6. Brain activity present 7. All systems in place 8. Appearance complete 9. Now officially a fetus 10. Just need to develop and increase size

(Contd...)

3rd	1. Length 9 cm and weight around 80 gm 2. Fingers are well separated 3. Nails begin to appear on finger and toes 4. Placenta is formed
4th	1. Length 16 cm and weight around 200 gm 2. Sex is distinguishable 3. Lanugo (soft hair) on the body 4. Head erect 5. External ears formed 6. Heart beat is loud enough to be heard with a stethoscope
5th	1. Length 25 cm and weight around 400 gm 2. Chalk like material (Vernix aseosa) appears upon the body 3. Fine hair on the scalp. 4. Vocal cords work; fetus can cry 5. Fetal movements felt by the mother
6th	1. Length 30 cm and weight around 900 gm 2. Hair appear on the head 3. Eyelids and eyelashes begun to form 4. Eyelids are closed 5. Navel is situated a little above pubis 6. Testicles lies close to kidney
7th	1. Length 35 cm and weight around 1.5 kg 2. Nails do not extended upto the tips of fingers and toes 3. Eyelids are open 4. Testicles are the external inguinal rings 5. Fetus is viable, i.e. can survives ex-utero
8th	1. Length 40 cm and weight around 2 kg 2. Lanugo disappear from face 3. Nails reaches to the tips of the fingers and the toes 4. Left testicles descended in to scrotum
9th	1. Length 48-52 cm and weight- 2-3 kg 2. Scalp covered with hair 2-3 cm in length 3. Nails have grown over the tip of the finger and toes 4. Both testicles descend into scrotum or labia has closed the vulva

CHILDBIRTH

In normal cases, after an average period of 9-month ± 10 days, a successful pregnancy terminates into the birth of child. Childbirth is also a lengthy procedure and takes around 14 hours (1st pregnancy) or 8 hours (subsequent pregnancy) and it includes three stages:

- Labor (the process of birth)
- Delivery (the birth itself)
- After Birth (Expulsion of placenta and fetal membranes)

First Stage of Labor

This is a very early and usually very slow stage. Cervix starts to open (dilate) due to progressive contractions of uterus. Cervix opens up to 10 cm diameter at the end of process:

In this stage women are quite. Woman is usually encouraged to walk in labor room to stimulate the process. It has following steps:

- As labor begins, womb (uterus) of the women begins to contract as the cervix relaxes and expands.
- Due to abdominal pressure, a watery bag (amniotic sac) surrounding the baby is pushed into the opening of cervix and it bursts. This process also known as "breaking of the bag of waters".
- Gradually abdominal contractions intensify the pressure against cervix.
- These contractions also make the cervix thin and to stretch open.
- Some drugs may be used to enhance uterine contraction, if these are not forceful enough to open the cervix.

  Pain killers are not recommended at this point because it slows down the labour process.
- At the end of first stage, uterine contractions are longer, more regular and painful, usually occurring about after every two minutes.
- At the end of this process cervix is dilated up to 10 cm.

- The child's head begins to come down and women begin to feel the urge to push down.

Be careful, and wait for the signal of pushing from maternity practitioner, otherwise early pushing can cause the cervix to swell and or to tear and bleed.

Second Stage of Labor

- At the beginning of this stage, baby's head appears at the top of the cervix.
- Uterine contractions get stronger.
- With the help of uterine (abdominal) contractions, woman starts pushing the infant down through the vagina.
- Baby's head appearing at the vaginal os is the sign of impending delivery.
- Through the pubic bone, head passes out first followed by shoulders and then the rest of the body.
- After the delivery umbilical cord is cut.

After Birth (Expulsion of Placenta and Fetal Membranes)

This is the last stage of labour; the placenta is pushed out from the vagina by the continuing uterine contractions. A regular contraction of uterus helps in the separation of placenta which is essential after normal delivery.

Contraception

1

Choices for Family Planning

During ancient times, sexual abstinence and withdrawal method were mainly used as the birth control method. In modern society due to the vast variety of contraceptives available, the sexual abstinence and withdrawal have very little value. There is no doubt that the dominant effect of the western culture is now increasingly visible in the Indian society. Non-vaginal sex is another type of sexual act having no risk of unwanted pregnancy. It includes forms of sex, such as the outercourse (sex without penetration), anal sex and oral sex.

Once the relationship between the release of semen into the vagina and the onset of pregnancy was known, some sexual partners began to use this as the best basis for the techniques for contraception. Sexual abstinence is the practice of refraining from all sexual activity. Withdrawal also known as the *coitus interruptus* methods, is the practice of ending sexual intercourse ("pulling out") before ejaculation. The main risk of coitus interruptus is that the man may not perform the manouvre correctly, or may not perform the manoeuvre in a timely manner. Although it is commonly believed that pre-ejaculate fluid can cause pregnancy, modern research has shown that pre-ejaculate fluid does not contain much viable sperms.

It was observed that following misconceptions and urban legends have given rise to a great deal of false claims. It must be kept in mind that:

- Passing urine after sex does not prevent pregnancy and is not a form of birth control, although it is often advised anyway to help prevent urinary tract infections.
- Douching with any substance immediately following intercourse acts as a contraceptive is wrong. While it may seem like a sensible idea to try to wash the ejaculate out of the vagina, it is not likely to be effective. Due to the nature of the fluids and the structure of the female reproductive tract — if anything, douching spreads semen further towards the uterus. Some slight spermicidal effect may occur if the douche solution is particularly acidic, but overall it is not scientifically observed to be a reliable and effective method of birth control.
- It is a myth that a female cannot become pregnant as a result of the first sexual intercourse.
- No sexual position prevents pregnancy but some sex positions may encourage pregnancy. Having sex while standing up or with a woman on top will not keep the sperm from entering the uterus. The force of ejaculation, the contractions of the uterus caused by prostaglandins in the semen, as well as ability of sperm to swim overrides gravity.
- Women are usually less fertile for the first few days after menstruation.
- Having sex in a hot tub does not prevent pregnancy, but may contribute to vaginal infections.

Instead of sexual abstinence, withdrawal and outercourse, different types of contraceptive methods of birth control are available are listed below. Characteristics of these methods and branded contraceptive available in the market are discussed further in this book.

1. Condoms
2. Birth Control Pills
3. Intrauterine Contraceptives
4. Injectable Contraceptives
5. Spermicidal Contraceptive (Suppositories Foams Sponges)
6. Female Condoms
7. Contraceptive Implants
8. Emergency Contraceptive Techniques

2

Condom

The male condom is a thin sheath that fits over a man's erect penis during intercourse. It is considered to be an effective over-the-counter, barrier method of reversible birth control. The condom is the only available method of birth control used by men other than the surgical operation (vasectomy). Their main advantage is easy availability, and ease of application. They are the only form of protection that can help both to stop the transmission of the sexually transmitted diseases (STDs) such as HIV as well as prevent pregnancy.

For the condoms, the prescribed national standards are minimum length (17.5 cms), unstretched width (4.4 cms), thickness (0.07 mm) and total weight of 1.7 grams. It's not clear whether latex or polyurethane condoms are stronger—there are studies suggesting that either of them is less likely to break. With both types, the likelihood of breakages is very small if used correctly. Various branded condoms use various types of lubricants and the lubrication on condoms also varies. Some condoms are not lubricated at all, some are lubricated with a silicone substance, and some condoms have a water-based lubricant. The lubrication on condoms aims to make the condom easier to put on and more comfortable to use. It can also help prevent condom breakage.

On the basis of material used in the manufacturing of the condom, three types of condoms are available in the market:

1. Condoms are usually made of latex or polyurethane. If possible one should use a latex condom, as they are slightly more reliable, and in most countries they are most readily available. Latex condoms can only be used with water based lubricants, not oil based lubricants such as Vaseline or cold cream as they break down the latex. A small number of people have an allergic reaction to latex and can use polyurethane condoms instead.
2. Polyurethane condoms are made of a type of plastic. They are thinner than latex condoms, and so they increase sensitivity and are more appealing for the feeling and appearance to some users. They are more expensive than latex condoms and slightly less flexible so more lubrication may be needed. However both oil and water based lubricants can be used with them.
3. Condoms of natural skin (lambskin) are also available that can help prevent a pregnancy, but not STDs, because these condoms have natural pores that allow bacteria and viruses (including HIV) to pass through.

Advantages of Using a Condom

- Prevents the spread of sexually transmitted infections, including HIV and AIDS.
- Easy birth control technique and easy to use.
- Available without a prescription.
- No hormonal side effects.
- Use can be part of sex play.
- Does not affect future fertility.
- May decrease women's risk for developing pre-cancerous cells on the cervix.

Disadvantages of Using a Condom

- Some people are allergic to latex. Polyurethane condoms can be used as an alternative.
- Some individuals argue that condoms reduce sensitivity and pleasure during intercourse.

- Condoms may break or leak if they are put on incorrectly.
- Must be readily available.
- Can interrupt sex play.

Things One Should Know

- Do not use two condoms at the same time. Male condoms and female condoms should not be used at the same time.
- Placing two male condoms on a penis can raise the chance of tearing.
- Condoms should not be used with oil-based lubricants such as petroleum jelly, vaseline, or mineral and vegetable oil. Such lubricants damage the condom.

Selection of an appropriate condom is a big problem, so it is suggested that one should look at the greatest selection of condoms, in term of style and size, given at the end of this chapter and also on Internet rather than in medical stores. For promoting the wide use of condom, a slogan is widely used "Condom, Bindass bol" to remove any hesitation in purchase of the condom. But at the time of purchases, some people immediately put into their pocket to hide without proper checking. So please be careful about the following points:

Points to be Considered While Choosing Condom Types

1. **Expiry date:** Condoms have expiry (Exp) and manufacturing (MFG) date on the box and on each condom's individual package. A condom used after the expiry date is more likely to tear or break.
2. **Look at the labeling**: make sure to read the condom label to check if it is FDA-approved for use against unplanned pregnancy and STDs. According to FDA regulations, anything that "sufficiently resembles" a condom must comply with FDA standards — including novelty condoms, like those that glow in the dark or are flavored. If condoms do not comply with these standards, they may not claim to be a contraceptive device.

3. **Texture:** Condoms are also available with various textures, such as ribs, bumps/studs, or a combination of both. The positioning of the ribs and/or bumps are designed to maximize pleasure for either or both partners.
4. **Strength:** Condoms come in regular strength and thicker strength. Some people may prefer thicker condoms (sometimes called extra strong or ultra strong), believing that these are more effective. Thinner condoms tend to allow more sensation. As long as the condom is FDA approved, either strength is equally effective.
5. **Size:** There is no standard length for condoms, but the one's made from latex rubber can stretch to fit the length of a man's erect penis. Condom widths can vary; there is about a 1.5 cm difference between the smallest and largest condom. A condom that is too small and tight may tear, and one that is too big may be more likely to slip off. One may have to experiment to find one that works for them. Smaller, 'closer' fit condoms are typically labeled trim or snug fit. One may find larger condoms labeled as XL, XXL or Magnum. Avanti brand condoms tend to be the largest and least tight.
6. **Lubrication:** Condoms can come "wet" (with lubrication) or dry (non-lubricated). Lubrication can help prevent condom breakage, and many people prefer lubricated condoms because they may make sex more comfortable. Keep in mind, only water-based or silicone-based lubrication can be used with latex condoms. Some condoms are lubricated with the spermicide nonoxynol-9; only use these condoms if you are not allergic to nonoxynol-9. If you are, it is possible to have a reaction resulting in little sores (which can make the transmission of HIV more likely).
7. **Shape:** There are many styles of condoms. They may be regular shaped (with straight sides), form-fitting (indented below the head of the penis), or they may be

flared (wider over the head of the penis). The differences in shape are designed to suit various personal preferences and enhance pleasure. Condoms can also have different tips, including a reservoir tip, a plain tip, a spiral tip and an over-sized tip.

8. **Novelty condoms:** These are special condoms usually intended more for fun and sex play, and they do not usually offer any protection against STDs or pregnancy. These condoms should be labeled 'FOR NOVELTY USE ONLY.

Types of Condoms Available in Local Market

1. Colored Condom
2. Contour Condom
3. Dotted Condom
4. Delay Condom
5. Latex Condom
6. Lubricated Condom
7. Passion Condom
8. Ribbed Condom
9. Ultra thick Condom
10. Ultra lubricated Condom
11. Ultra-thin Condom
12. Vibrating Condom
13. Warming Condom
14. Wave-ribbed Condom
15. Fragrances Condom

Some Famous Brands of Condom

1. Kohinoor
2. Kamasutra
3. Moods
4. Kobra
5. Masti
6. Durex

3

The Pill

Birth control pills, also called Combined Oral Contraceptive Pill (COCP), contain hormones similar to the natural hormones in a female's body like estrogen and progesterone. Since last 50 years, this is the most popular and reversible method of contraception world-wide. There are two kinds of pills i.e.:

1. Combination pills or combined pills (COCP)
2. Mini pills.

The COCP often referred to as "The Pill", is a combination of an estrogen (oestrogen) and a progestin (progestogen), taken by mouth to inhibit normal female fertility. However, 99 per cent of all pills are combination pills, which contain both estrogen and progesterone. The mini pill is so-called because it contains only progesterone.

If woman is starting on birth control pills, she should start them on the fifth day of her period, regardless of whether bleeding has stopped. Used in combination or alone, these hormones prevent pregnancy by:

- Preventing ovulation.
- Keeping the mucus in the cervix thick, so sperms cannot penetrate it.
- Preventing a fertilized egg from implanting in the endometrium (uterine lining).

Advantages of Oral Contraceptives Pills

- Simple and easily available and very effective when used properly.
- Can be used as long as a woman wants to prevent pregnancy.
- Pills can be stopped at any time.
- No need to do any thing at the time of sexual intercourse.
- Fertility returns soon after stopping pills.
- Menstrual cycles are regular, lesser bleeding, fewer days of bleeding and milder cramps.
- Can be used as long as a woman wants to prevent pregnancy.
- Can be used by any woman irrespective of whether she has children or not.

Uses of Various Pills

1. Combined Contraceptive Pills

Various combined oral contraceptive pills come in packages of 21 or 28 pills. If the pack contains 21 pills, then the woman should take the pill each day, at roughly the same time, for 21 days. She should then stop taking the pill for 7 days (during which she will most likely menstruate) and then start again on the next pack of 21 pills. If the pack contains 28 pills, the woman is expected to have a pill for 28 days, and then without missing a day, start with the next pack (regardless of her periods). The reason is that the pack of 28 pills contains not only 21 hormone pills, but also 7 'blank' pills with no active ingredients. If she forget to take one pill then take two pills the next day. If she miss two pills in the third week of the pill pack, then start a new pack immediately because this is your fertile period.

2. Mini Pills or Pills for Breast-feeding Mothers (Progestogen only Pill)

These types of birth control pills are prescribed to the breast-feeding mothers because combined pills may affect the quality as well as the quantity of the breast milk.

These are also prescribed to the woman who has severe side effects with combined pills. These pills are devoid of estrogen, therefore they do not cause estrogen related side effects. Progesterone related side effects are also less because these pills contain lesser amount of progesterone. With this therapy ovulation continues to occur in 70 per cent of cycles. Contraceptive effects are due to the alteration in the cervical mucus and endometrium.

Progesterone pills contain only low doses of progesterone alone. This involves daily dosage with norethisterone 350µg, dinorgestrel 75µg, ethynodiol diacetate 500 µg or L-norgestrol 30 µg with no break in medication.

Some Common Problems Associated with the Use of the Pills and Their Solutions

Side effects of these pills are observed in approximately 5 per cent of the users. Some common side effects are nausea, vomiting, intermenstrual bleeding, mild headaches, breast tenderness; sometimes, amenorrhoea, slight weight gain, depression; rarely, hepatic disease and very rarely stroke or heart attack in women with high blood pressure, more than 35 years of age and heavy smokers.

They should be reassured that these side effects are not serious and usually disappear or their intensity decreases within three to four months after starting the pills. Woman should not skip pills. For common side effects, they should be advised of following measures:

- **Nausea and vomiting:** She should take the pills at night or with meals.
- **Headache:** She can take paracetamol and other pain killer. If headache is too severe she may switch over to progesterone only pill.

- **Breast tenderness:** This is due to progestogenic side effects of the combined contraceptive pills. If it persists for more than six months change over to more estrogenic pills (sequential pill).
- **Weight gain:** It is due to fluid retention and/or mild anabolic effects. In 4 -50 per cent of cases weight gain occurs in early months but tend to settle spontaneously within a year.
- **Libido:** Usually contraceptive pills do not show any changes. Due to some psychological factors, it may increase or decrease in some women.
- **Amenorrhoea (no monthly bleedings):** Reassure her and ask her to start the next packet on its usual time. It may improve by giving her more estrogenic preparation.
- **Break through bleeding:** Reassure her that periods usually regularize in three months. Breakthrough bleeding is more with progestin only pills.
- **Menorrhagia (excessive bleeding during periods):** She should take more progestrogenic prepration.
- **Ovarian cysts:** These are more common among women taking progestin only pills. These are not pathological cysts. These are actually follicles (small fluid filled structure in the ovary) that continues grow beyond the size in a normal menstrual cycle. They usually disappear on their own. They may cause some abdominal pain but rarely require treatment.
- **Abdominal pain in progestin only user:** Rarely but in few cases due to ectopic pregnancy, it cause severe abdominal pain and sometimes fainting attack. It is life threatening condition and requires immediate treatment or hospitalization.

Uses of Contraceptive Pill in Some Special Cases

Hypertensive cases: Estrogen containing pill slightly enhance blood pressure but it is reversible. If blood pressure is within the normal range (140-90 mm Hg), pill can be given safely. But if blood pressure is recorded between 140-160 mm Hg and 90-100 mm Hg, pills can be given with cautions, if patients refers to this method only, but regular checking of blood pressure is required (once a week).

If it increases or remains on higher side pills should be discontinued. If blood pressure is more than 160/100 mm Hg pills are not given.

Smokers: Women less than 35 years of age can take low dose combined oral pills. Elder smokers can take pills if they stop smoking. Older women who cannot stop smoking and prefer pills, must take progestin only pills.

Older women in this case can also use post coital pills because preventing pregnancy is more important in such patients.

Some Misconceptions Regarding the Pills

Regarding fertility: There is no subsequent effect on fertility. 70 per cent of women resume normal ovulatory cycles in the first post treatment cycle, 95 per cent within first three post menstrual cycles, if their pre-treatment fertility was normal. Only few women have to wait for six or more months for normal menstrual periods to return.

Regarding baby: There is no effect on child, if conception takes place after a woman stop taking pills. Even if a woman takes some pills accidentally while pregnant, they will not make the baby deformed.

Cancer: They have not been proved to cause any cancer.

Various Contents of Contraceptive Pills

Estrogen: The estrogens used are ethinyl estradiol or its 3-methyl ether derivatives-mestranol. At low dosage, ethinyl estradiol is more potent than mestranol.

Progestogens: The progestogens fall under the following chemical categories:

1. **19-nortestosterone derivatives**: These are ethisterone, dimethisterone, norethisterone or norethindrone, norethidrone acetate, ethynodiol diacetate, norethynodrel, nestrenol, norgestrel and desogestel.

Norgestrel is the most potent progestogen in this series. These compounds are somewhat estrogenic because they either metabolize or have inherent estrogenic properties. These are most the powerful ovulation inhibitors.

2. **17-alpha hydroxyprogesterone derivatives:** These are 17-acetoxyprogesterone, medroxyprogesterone acetate, megestrol acetate and chlormadinone acetate. This group of compound does not have any estrogenic activity and these are less powerful ovulation inhibitors.
3. **Long acting derivatives:** Introduction of cyclopentyl ether group at position either in a ethinyl estradiol or a 19-norethesterone derivative produces long acting hormones namely quinestrol and quingestanol respectively.

Mechanism of Action

Combined oral contraceptive pills were developed to prevent ovulation by progestogenic and estrogenic suppression of gonadotropin release. Combined hormonal contraceptives, including COCPs, inhibit follicular development and prevent ovulation as their primary mechanism of action.

Progestogen negative feedback decreases the pulse frequency of gonadotropin-releasing hormone (GnRH) released by the hypothalamus, which in turn decreases the release of follicle-stimulating hormone (FSH) and greatly decreases the release of luteinizing hormone (LH) by the anterior pituitary. Decreased levels of FSH inhibit follicular development, preventing an increase in estradiol levels. Progestogen negative feedback and the lack of estrogen positive feedback on LH release prevent a mid-cycle LH surge. Inhibition of follicular development and the absence of a LH surge prevents ovulation.

Estrogen was originally included in oral contraceptives for better cycle control (to stabilize the endometrium and thereby reduce the incidence of breakthrough bleeding), but was also found to inhibit follicular development and help prevent ovulation. Estrogen negative feedback on the anterior pituitary greatly decreases the release of FSH, which inhibits follicular development and helps prevent ovulation.

A secondary mechanism of action of all progestogen-containing contraceptives is the inhibition of sperm penetration through the cervix into the upper genital tract (uterus and fallopian tubes) by decreasing the amount and increasing the viscosity of the cervical mucus.

Other secondary mechanisms have been hypothesized. One example is endometrial effects, which prevents implantation of an embryo in the uterus. Pro-life groups consider such a mechanism to be abortifacient, and the existence of post fertilization mechanisms is a controversial topic. Some scientists point out that the possibility of fertilization during COCP use is very small. From this, they conclude that endometrial changes are unlikely to play an important role, if any, in the observed effectiveness of COCPs.

Non-Hormonal Oral Contraceptives (Centchroman)

It is a non-hormonal contraceptive which is developed indigenously. It is free from estrogenic side effects of hormonal contraceptives.

Dosage: First tablet (dose of 30 mg) used on first day of menstrual cycle and thereafter twice a week for three months, followed by once a week. Consult your doctor for any contraindication like cervical hyperplasia, polycystic ovarian diseases, nursing mothers up to 1st six months etc.

Daily Pills Combined Oral Contraceptives

Sl. No.	Brand Name	Company	Composition	Pills/ Pack	Rate Rs.
1	Mala-N	Indo Drug Pharma	Levonorgestrel+Ethinyl oestradiol	28	Govt. supply (free)
2	Mala-D	Indo Drug Pharma	Levonorgestrel+Ethinyl oestradiol	28	3.00
3	Pearl	Femi Care Ltd	Levonorgestrel+Ethinyl oestradiol	28	5.00

Daily Pills Combined Oral Contraceptives

Sl No.	Brand Name	Company	Composition	Pills/ Pack	Rate (Rs.)
1.	Femilon	Organon	Ethinyloestradiol+ Desogestral	21	102.75
2.	Novelon	Organon	Ethinyloestradiol+ Desogestral	21	89.50
3.	Perilon	Par Lab	Ethinyloestradiol+ Desogestral	21	85.00
4.	Perilon-D	Par Lab	Ethinyloestradiol+ Desogestral	21	96.80
5.	Cojugase	Elder	Conjugated oestrogens	28	220.00
6.	Espauz	Glenmark	Conjugated Oestrogens	28	203.00
7.	Premarin	Wyeth	Conjugated Oestrogens	28	390.00
8.	Progynova	Zydus	Ethinyloestradiol	21	137.00
9.***	Contra-P	Par Lab	Levonorgestrel+Ethinyl oestradiol	21	55.00
10.***	Duoluton-L	Cadila/GR	Levonorgestrel+Ethinyl oestradiol	21	51.98
11.***	Ovral	Wyith	Levonorgestrel+Ethinyl oestradiol	21	50.00
12.***	Regcyl	DPPL	Levonorgestrel+Ethinyl oestradiol	21	30.00
13.**	Ovral-L	Wyith	Levonorgestrel+Ethinyl oestradiol	21	62.00
14.**	Ovral-G	Wyith	Coby + Norgestrel		
15.*	Loette	Wyith	Levonorgestrel+Ethinyl oestradiol	21	99.50
16.*	Lo-stren	DPPL	Levonorgestrel+Ethinyl oestradiol	21	30.00
17.*	Contra-S	Par Lab	Levonorgestrel+Ethinyl oestradiol	21	45.00
18.@	Dronis-20	Sloectra	Drospiezenoue + Ethinyl oestradiol	24/4	—

Mini Pills

Sl. No.	Brand Name	Company	Composition	Pills/ Pack	Rate (Rs.)
1.	Zerogen	Organone/gsk	Desogestral	28	223.00
2.	Intimacy	Otsiragenetic	Desogestral	28	180.00

Non-Hormonal Oral Contraceptives

Sl. No.	Brand Name	Company	Pills/ Pack	Rate (Rs.)
1.	Centron	Torrent	8	12.00
2.	Saheli	Hindustan Latex Ltd.	8	16.00

*** High-Dose Oral Contraceptive pills

** Medium Dose Oral Contraceptive pills

*Low Dose Oral Contraceptive pills

@Low Dose Oral Contraceptive pill

(*For WHO Guidelines, see page nos. 202, 203*)

4

Intrauterine Device (IUD) Contraception

An intrauterine device (IUD) is a small device which is placed into the uterine cavity. Presently IUDs are small, safe, relatively inexpensive, and provide an extremely effective long-term contraception. An IUD is a small, T-shaped plastic device that is wrapped in copper or contains hormones. The IUD is inserted into uterus by the health professional. There are different types and sizes of IUD to suit different women. It has one or two soft threads or plastic strings tied to the end of the IUD which hangs down through the cervix into the vagina. One can check that the IUD is in place by feeling this string. The string is also used by a health professional to remove the IUD.

Users can get intrauterine contraception from the clinicians, health department, or the family planning clinic. ***Most clinics insert intrauterine contraceptive when a woman is in her periods or within 7 days of the start of the period.*** The IUD is fitted inside the womb. Fitting an IUD takes about 15–20 minutes. It can be uncomfortable or painful for some women, and she might want to use pain relieving drugs or a local anesthetic. The doctor or nurse will examine her internally to find the position and size of her womb before they put in an IUD. Sometimes they will check for any possible existing infections. It is better to do this before the IUD is put in. In some circumstances woman may be given antibiotics at the same time as the IUD is fitted. She may get a period like pain and some light bleeding for a few days after the IUD is fitted. Pain relief can help with this.

An IUD can be put in within 48 hours of birth, and usually it is put within four weeks after a vaginal or caesarean birth. It is advised that she uses some other method of contraception for three weeks (till day 21) after the birth or until the IUD is put in. An IUD can be put in by an experienced doctor or nurse immediately after a miscarriage or abortion if a woman was pregnant for less than 5 months. Most women who want to use an IUD can do so, including women who have never been pregnant and women who are HIV positive. But IUD is not recommended for those who are suffering from the following problems:

- An untreated sexually transmitted infection or pelvic infection and also when both partners are at risk of getting a sexually transmitted infection.
- Unexplained bleeding from the vagina (for example between periods or after sex).
- Problems with your womb or cervix.
- Woman suspects that, she might be already pregnant.

Advantages of an IUD

- It works as soon as it is put in.
- It works for 5–10 years, depending upon the type.
- It doesn't interrupt sex.
- It can be used if you are breastfeeding.
- Her normal fertility returns as soon as the IUD is taken out.
- It is not affected by other medicines.

Disadvantages of an IUD

- Periods may be heavier, longer or more painful. This may improve after a few months.

- She will need an internal examination to check if it is suitable, and when it is fitted.
- The IUD does not protect her from sexually transmitted infections, so she may have to use condoms as well. If she get an infection when an IUD is in place this could lead to a pelvic infection if it is not treated.

User should be Careful Regarding the Following Facts

- She may have some slight bleeding between her first two or three periods after she has had the IUD fitted. Many women have heavier, longer and more painful periods.
- If she has prolonged bleeding it may be possible for the doctor or nurse to give her additional medicine that can help control the bleeding. They may also check that the bleeding is not due to other causes such as infection.
- There is a very small chance of getting an infection during the first 20 days after an IUD is put in. She may be advised to have a check for any possible existing infections before an IUD is fitted.
- The IUD can be pushed out by one's womb (expulsion) or it can move (displacement). This is not common, and more likely to happen soon after it has been put in and she may not know it has happened. This is why her doctor or nurse will teach her how to check own IUD threads every month.
- It is not common, but there is a risk that an IUD might go through (perforate) one's womb or cervix when it is put in. This may cause pain but often there are no symptoms. If it happens, the IUD may have to be removed by surgery. The risk of perforation is low when an IUD is fitted by an experienced doctor or nurse.
- The risk of ectopic pregnancy is less in women using an IUD than in the women using no contraception at all. If one do become pregnant while she is using an IUD

there is a small increased risk of her having an ectopic pregnancy. If there is a sudden or unusual pain in the lower abdomen, seek medical advice as soon as possible.

- It is very unlikely that an IUD will come out, but if she cannot feel the threads, or if she thinks, she can feel the IUD itself, she may not be protected against pregnancy. Consult the doctor or nurse straightaway and use an extra contraceptive method, such as condoms. If she had sex recently, she might need to use emergency contraception.

Emergency Contraception

If woman has sex without using contraception or think her method might have failed there are two emergency methods she can use:

- The emergency hormonal pill — must be taken within three days (72 hours) after sex. The earlier it is taken after sex, the more it is effective.
- An IUD — must be fitted up to five days after sex, or up to five days after the earliest time you could have released an egg (ovulation).

Ask the doctor or nurse about getting emergency pills in advance, just in case she needs them.

To Remove IUD

It is important to note that IUDs do not disintegrate or split up and, for the most part, will not come out on their own and after a particular time, a woman must have an IUD removed. An IUD can be removed at anytime during the menstrual cycle. However, studies have shown that it may be a ***little easier to remove an IUD during menstruation because the cervix is naturally softened at that time.***

The procedure of an IUD removal is often easier, less painful, and quicker than the insertion. ***But it is especially important to note that a woman should never try to remove her IUD by herself or ask an unqualified person to do so as***

this could cause serious damage. A woman may have several reasons, why she would want her IUD removed such as:

- When the IUD is no longer effective.
- Wants to become pregnant.
- The development of an infection.
- Continual side effects that a woman can no longer tolerate.
- A woman may just not like it.

Types of IUD

There are two broad categories of intrauterine contraceptive devices:

1. Inert and copper-based devices.
2. Hormonal-based (progestogen releasing) devices.

Both types of IUD prevents fertilization of the egg by damaging or killing sperms. The IUD also affects the uterine lining (where a fertilized egg would implant and grow).

Copper is toxic to sperm. It makes the uterus and fallopian tubes produce fluid that kills sperms. This fluid contains white blood cells, copper ions, enzymes, and prostaglandins. Hormone-based IUD prevents fertilization by damaging or killing sperm and making the mucus in the cervix thick and sticky, so sperm can't get through to the uterus. It also keeps the lining of the uterus (endometrium) from becoming very thick. This makes the lining a poor place for a fertilized egg to implant and grow. The hormones in the LNG IUD also relieve irregular menstrual bleeding and cramp.

The Copper-T IUD

In the horizontal arms of the Copper T 380A IUD there is some copper. The IUD slowly gives off copper into the uterine cavity. This does several things. Most importantly, it stops the sperms from making their way up through the uterus. Among all the couples who use this IUD, only less than 1 per cent of them will experience an accidental pregnancy in the first year.

Advantages of the Copper-T IUD

- The Copper-T IUD is the second most effective reversible method, rivaling surgical sterilization in preventing pregnancy.
- The IUD is effective for at least 10 years.
- Only 2 of 100 women using a Copper T for 10 years will become pregnant.
- Prevents ectopic pregnancies.
- Far more readily reversible than tubal sterilization or vasectomy.
- Protects against endometrial cancer.
- Very low cost over time, Convenient, Safe, and Private.
- Non-hormonal IUD's are considered safe for use while breastfeeding.

Disadvantages of the Copper-T IUD

- No protection against sexually transmitted infections. Use condoms if there is any risk.
- There may be cramping, pain or spotting after insertion.
- The number of bleeding days is slightly higher than normal and she could have somewhat increased menstrual cramping. If one's bleeding pattern is bothersome to her, contact the clinician. There are medications which may make the woman have a more acceptable pattern of bleeding.
- High initial cost of insertion.
- Must be inserted by a doctor, medical practitioner, nurse midwife or physician's assistant.
- A small percentage of women are allergic to copper.

The LNG-IUS

Usually called "fit and forget" method and also makes female's periods lighter and shorter. The contraceptive is quite small (about 11/4'' tall and wide), made of plastic, and shaped like the letter "T". The LNG-IUS contains some levonorgestrel in its vertical arm. This hormone is a progestin, much like the progesterone a woman's ovaries produce in each monthly cycle. Each week the LNG-IUS gives off about the same amount of levonorgestrel as a woman gets when she takes one or two of the minipills called Ovrette. The levonorgestrel causes the cervical mucus to become thicker so that sperms cannot reach the egg. Among typical couples who initiate use of the LNG-IUS, just one in 1,000 women will experience an accidental pregnancy in the first year. It is best for those who have normal uterus.

Advantages of the LNG-IUS

- The LNG-IUS is the most effective reversible method, rivaling surgical sterilization in preventing pregnancy.
- It prevents ectopic pregnancies and pelvic inflammatory disease, decreases menstrual cramping and dramatically decreases menstrual blood loss (up to a 97 per cent reduction in menstrual blood loss according to one study).
- It may be left in place for up to seven years.
- It is safe, inexpensive over time, and provides extremely effective long-term contraception from a single insertion.
- One of the costs of any contraceptive is the cost to you should your contraceptive fail. Given the extremely low failure rate of the LNG-IUS, a person using this method is far less likely to have either the emotional and financial expenses associated with an unintended pregnancy.

Disadvantages of the LNG-IUS

- It often changes the menstrual cycle. A woman has more bleeding days than normal for the first few months and less than normal after six to eight months. If a woman finds that her bleeding pattern is bothersome, she should contact a clinician. Some medications may improve the pattern of bleeding.

- This method provides no protection against sexually transmitted infections. Use condoms to improve protection against sexually transmitted infections.
- It has a high initial cost of insertion.

Some Branded IUD

Sl. No.	Brand	Company	Specification	Safety period	Price (Rs.)
1.	Mirena	G. Reme	Levonorgestrel IUS	10 years	7591.00
2.	Multiload (Cu-250)	Organon	IUD for uteri with sound Length 6-9 cm	3 years	295.00
3.	Multiload (Cu-375)	Organon	IUD for uteri with sound Length 6-9 cm	5 years	442.00
4.	U-Kare	DKT India	IUD having 350 sp mm of copper surface area	5 years	200.00
5.	Zicoid	Cadila	IUD having 350 sp mm of copper surface area	5 years	195.00
6.	Zyload	Zydus Cadila	IUD for parous and multiparous women		249.00
7.	Cu-T200 (Gynae-7)		IUD having 200 mm of copper surface area 3.6 cm length	3-4 years	Free (Govt. supply)
8.	Cu-T380 A		IUD having 380 mm of copper surface area	10 years	"

(*For WHO guidelines, see page no. 204*)

5

Contraceptive Injection

Taking contraceptive pills is a dedicated task and the users are very conscious about it. Even sometimes ladies take it as a daily burden. Contraceptives injections are very similar to hormonal pills and also have same physiological action in the human body. But most important thing about the injections is that, if woman takes injection, she will be free from the daily burden of pills for one to several months. The injection is a long-acting reversible method of contraception. All long-acting methods are very effective because while they are being used woman do not have to remember to take or use contraception.

Injectable contraceptives are used as a temporary method of contraception by females. They have been in use in India since 1992. There are two types of contraceptive injections available in the market i.e. contraceptive injections containing only progestogen hormone which is similar to the natural progesterone that women produce in their ovaries and secondly, similar to the combined oral birth control pills, combined contraceptive injections containing a combination of synthetic estrogen and progestin.

Like all other injections, these injections are also injected into the muscles of the upper arm, thigh, or buttocks. This injection is NOT to be massaged. However, woman could apply light pressure to the injected area for 1-2 minutes. After each shot, the hormone levels peak and gradually decrease until the next injection.

Action Mechanism

Similar to the contraceptive pills it also has the following mode of action:

- Stop the ovulation (releasing an egg monthly from the ovary).
- Thicken the mucus from the cervix. This makes it difficult for sperm to move through it and reach an egg.
- Make the lining of your womb thinner, so it is less likely to accept a fertilized egg.

Advantages of Contraceptive Injections

- Woman does not have to remember to take a pill every day.
- She have only to think about contraception every 2-3 months.
- It does not interfere with sex.
- It can be used when breastfeeding.
- It may help some of the problems of periods, such as pre-menstrual tension, heavy periods, and pain.
- It can be used by some women who cannot take the combined pills (which contains oestrogen).
- It may help protect against pelvic infection. (the mucus plug in the cervix may help stop bacteria travel into the uterus).

Disadvantages of Contraceptive Injections

- The injection cannot be removed once given, so its effect lasts 2-3 months. If side-effects occur there is little that can be done about them.
- Because the injection is long acting, it takes some time after the last injection for its effect to wear off. This time varies from woman to woman. Some women take 6-8 months after the last injection before fertility returns. Rarely, it can take up to 2 years before fertility returns. This delay is not related to the length of time for which you use this method of contraception.
- Woman periods are likely to change. During the first few months some women have irregular bleeding which can be heavier and longer than normal. But, it is unusual for the heavy periods to persist. After the first few months it is more common for the periods to become lighter than usual, although they may be irregular. Many women have no periods at all. The longer it is used, the more likely the periods will stop. Periods stop in about half of users within 12 months of use. Some women worry about changes to their periods, but they are of no consequence. However, unpredictable or irregular periods can be a nuisance.

Contraceptive Injections

These are of two types:

1. Progestin only
2. Combined Injectable Contraceptive (CIC), containing both progesterone and estradiol:

In India only progestin containing injectables are vastly used. There are 2 types of progestin only containing ICs available in the market. They are:

1. **Noristerat** (Chemical name—Norethindrone Enanthate, also called Net-en). Noristerat is to be given every 2 months.
2. **Depo Provera** (Chemical name—Medroxyprogesterone acetate).Depo Provera is to begiven every three months.

Combined injectable contraceptive (CIC) is the name of the monthly injection, containing progesterone and estradiol. This method of birth control must be administered every 28 to 30 days (and must not exceed 33 days following the date of the previous injection). When the prescribed dosing schedule is followed, combined contraceptive injections are considered to have a failure rate of less than 1 per cent each year.

Brand names include *Cyclofem*, *Novafem*, *Mesigyna*, *Lunelle*.

Cyclofem is also marketed as: Cyclofemina, Feminena, Novafem, Lunella, and Cyclo-Provera.

Mesigyna is also marketed as: Norigynon, Mesigyna Instayect, Mesygest, and No. 3 injectable Norigynon.

- *Cyclofem* contains depomedroxy-progesterone acetate (DMPA) 25 mg and estradiol cypionate 5 mg.
- *Mesigyna* contains norethisterone enanthate (NET EN) 50 mg and estradiol valerate 5 mg.
- *Lunelle* contains medroxyprogesterone acetate (MPA) 25 mg plus estradiol cypionate (E2C) 5 mg.
- *Deladroxate* contains dihydroxy-progesterone acetophenide 150 mg and estradiol enanthate 10 mg.

These are best if used between the 1st and 5th days of the menstrual cycle or immediately after the menstrual period. These may also be used anytime during the menstrual cycle, if the woman and her doctor are sure that she is not pregnant.

- Postpartum within 6 weeks after normal delivery or Caesarian delivery. This injection is NOT to be massaged. However, you could apply light pressure to the injected area for 1-2 minutes.
- Post abortion - immediately or within 7 days after abortion.

(*For WHO Guidelines, see page nos. 202, 203*)

6

Contraceptive Implant

Implants are the hormonal contraceptives, which require only 5 to 10 minutes of simple procedure for fitting. They provide protection for long duration (3-6 years depending upon the brand). Contraceptive implant works in a similar way to contraceptive pills but once you use implants, forget the burden of pills for at least three year.

These are small tubes (one or more) that are fitted or inserted under the skin of the upper arm by a doctor or nurse, local anesthetic is also applied to reduce the pain. The size of tube is around 40 mm and contains synthetic progesterone. They prevent pregnancy in multiple ways i.e.:

1. Prevent the release of an egg from the ovary.
2. Decrease the tubal (fallopian tube) motility.
3. Thinning of the womb lining (changing endometium) that is hostile for the implantation of fertilized egg.
4. Thickens and hardens cervical mucus to prevent the entry of sperms through cervix.
5. Slowly releases progestogens into your body to provide protection for longer duration.

Insertion of Contraceptives Implant

Implantation should be done between 5-10 days of menstruation cycle and ensure that woman is not pregnant. Implantation should be done by expert practitioner. Women should be aware about its advantage as well as disadvantage.

Prepare and encourage the candidate to keep the implant for at least three months under any circumstance and patients should consult properly with their physician about the problems arising from implantation.

There are Following Steps for the Insertion of the Implants

- It is put in the inner side of the upper arm (Between armpits and elbow).
- Use some local anesthesia near the site of insertion to reduce the pain of insertion.
- A small incision is made.
- A needle like part of carrier (loader) is inserted; doctor loads the implant into arm by pressing/clicking the non-needle like part of carrier.
- The wound is dressed and will soon heal just like any other small cut.
- There is no need for stitches or anything.

Removing Implants

After successful period, it should be removed with the help of expert doctors. Under local anesthesia, it needs a small surgical incision or operation to remove it and if women wish to put a new implant to repeat it. It is done simultaneously.

Woman can also remove the implant if she wants a baby.

Advantages of Contraceptives Implant

- If you adopt this method, forget the burden of daily pills or for at least three years.

- Best for woman who is unable to use combined oral pills containing estrogen.
- Don't like other contraceptive methods or find them unreliable.
- Rapidly effective (with in 24 hours).
- Also recommended for breast feeding females.
- Immediately return to fertility on removal.
- Due to psychological reasons women prefer implants as compared to the IUD (No need of any gynaecologist).
- Helps in protection from pelvic infection (The mucus plugs in the cervix may help to prevent bacteria from travelling into the uterus).
- Women lose less blood during menstruation.
- It is also beneficial for certain premenstrual symptoms like cramps, headaches, and breast tenderness.
- It can be removed if you have trouble with it, and you can get pregnant right after removal.
- Highly effective (0.05-1 pregnancies per 100 women during the first year of use).

Disadvantages of Contraceptives Implant

- Need a trained practitioner.
- Wound infection may occur at the place of insertion
- Following few problems are observed during the 1st year of insertion of implants:
  - Change in the pattern of menstruation (heavier, longer and irregular periods)
  - Change in mood and severe depression
  - Weight gain
  - Acne
- In some women the periods become infrequent and light, or even stop altogether.
- It can be difficult to remove.

- Migration of implant sticks also reported.
- You could experience some bruising, tenderness or swelling at the site where the implant was inserted.
- Some medicines or homeopathic remedies may reduce its effectiveness. Consult the doctor for more details.

Contraceptives Implant is not Recommended in the Following Cases

- Family history of any type of cancer.
- Continuous vaginal bleeding (unknown reason).
- Woman suffering from thrombosis (Thrombosis is the coagulation of blood in a blood vessel).
- Woman having severe liver disease.
- Woman suffering from jaundice.
- Females suffering from ovarian cyst.
- Woman suffering from tuberculosis and using following medicine such as rifampicin (Rifadin) and rifabutin (Mycobutin).
- Woman suffering from epilepsy and using phenytoin (Epanutin), carbamazepine (Tegretol), phenobarbital and primidone (Mysoline) medicines.

Management of some common side effects

Sl. No.	Side Effects	Managements
1.	Irregular or heavy bleeding	Check for gynecological problems Counseling and reassurance Provide COCs pills or pills contain strogens
2.	Headache	Analgesic pills
3.	Breast tenderness	Use appropriate bra
4.	Breast discharge	Decreased nipple stimulation
5.	Weight gain	Exercise, proper diet & consult dietician
6.	Acne	Diet, cleansers and antibiotic treatment

Types of contraceptive implants available

Sl. No.	Brand Name	No. of Rods	Contents	Manufacturer	Duration of action
1.	Implanon	1 Rod Sys	Levonorgestrel	Pop. council	3 years
2.	Jadelle	2 Rods Sys	Levonorgestrel	Pop. council	3 years
3.	Norplant	6 Rods Sys	Etonorgestrel	NV Organon	5 yrs (now 7 yrs)

(*For WHO Guidelines, see page nos. 202, 203*)

7

Spermicidal Contraceptives

Spermicidal agents are contraceptive used by females by placing these agents into their vagina shortly before sex. These are highly effective if used with the barrier methods (Cervical cap and Diaphragm). Unfortunately these barriers are not available in Indian market. Spermicidal agents are only available in the form of cream and vaginal pessaries.

Spermicidal contraceptive are best for following cases

- When some partner avoids barrier method due to pleasure or latex allergy.
- Reduced rate of sexual encounter and when couples also avoid hormonal contraceptive due to adverse effect on body.
- Women who cannot tolerate or object to using oral contraceptives or an IUD.
- Woman who needs infrequent protection and as an interim method for women who forget to take oral contraceptives or expel an IUD.
- Some unmarried couples, who also prefer this method.

- Woman who have reduced vaginal lubrication (vaginal cream enhance the lubrication).

Advantages of Spermicidal Contraceptives

- Provide safety from conception when required.
- No adverse side effect on body.
- No effect on mother's milk.
- Very easy to use with little practice.

Spermicidal Contraceptive

The vaginal spermicidal agents fight directly with the sperm like a soldier on the border. They are applied/ inserted near the cervix (opening of uterus) and prevent the entry and are toxic to sperms.

These agents are currently available in the form of foams, gels, creams, vaginal pessaries and water soluble film but only cream and vaginal pessaries are available in India. The agents should be placed in the vagina, 10-30 minutes before sex after carefully studying the specific instructions given by the manufacturer.

They prevent pregnancy in two different ways:

1. Their insertion in the vagina before sex produces a barrier for the sperm penetration into the uterus through the cervix.
2. Some spermicides have few active ingredients (for example nonoxynol-9) that are directly toxic to sperms, which immobilizes and kills them on contact. Few vaginal spermicides contain nonionic surfactants that directly act on the membrane of sperms and damage them.

After safe sex, douching should be done till 6-8 hours with fresh and/or clean water.

Some Disadvantages of Spermicidal Contraceptive

- Some time it may cause allergic reaction to partners, so test of allergic reaction should be done before use or keep some anti-allergic medicine during the first few sexual encounter.

- Can cause irritation to both partners, when it is used several time in a day.
- Precaution should be taken when using melting type of spermicidal (use between 20-50 minutes before sex) and should be kept (store) at cool and dry places.
- Some foaming tablets may cause warm sensation (don't worry)
- Some spermicides may be messy.
- Proper sanitation (cleaning) should be required during whole process. Hands should be clean before and after the use of these agents.
- Success rate is comparatively low (around 21 pregnancies out of 100 cases).

Spermicidal Preparations are Following Five Types

1. Suppositories
2. Creams/Jellies
3. Aerosol spray
4. Foam tablets
5. C-film

List of some of spermicidal contraceptives available in India

Sl. No.	Brand	Company	Form	Pack	Strength	Price (Rs.)
1.	Delfen	Jansen Cilag	Cream		Nonoxyphenoxy polyethoxy ethanol 5%	19.25
2.	Today	Bliss	Veg-Pess		Nonoxynol(9) 5%	19.70

8

Emergency and MT Pills

Contraceptives are used to prevent pregnancy. Emergency contraceptives are those contraceptives which provide you extra protection from unwanted pregnancy under following circumstances:

- Missing one's routinely used contraceptive.
- Condom leakage and breakage during sex.
- Improper use by some couples who are some times confused and do not know much regarding fertility awareness based methods for contraception.
- Unplanned/sudden sexual encounter.
- To avoid pregnancy after rape or forceful sexual encounter.

These contraceptives are effective after several hours/or few days after sex and there is no need to worry about the pregnancy, if used immediately after sex. These are used occasionally (not routinely) due to the above mentioned circumstances and they are not as effective as the condoms.

Some Facts About Emergency Contraceptives

- Use as early as possible.
- Effective only if used within 5 days after unprotected sex.
- Delay or prevent ovulation.

- Block implantation by preventing the attachment of a fertilized egg to the wall of the uterus (womb).
- Interrupting the production of hormones needed for the pregnancy to continue.
- ***Do not abort existing pregnancy.***
- Also have some effect upon the duration of next menstruation cycles (some female have early period and few have a late one).
- After the use of pill, if menstruation cycle is delayed by 7 or more days from expected time- go for pregnancy test.
- Withdrawal bleeding will occur in 3-7 days.

These pills are usually used by couple who had unprotected and unplanned sex and/or unmarried couples. For the practice of safe sex, adoption of the barrier (condom) methods is the best.

Some Hard Facts

1. These pills are 75 per cent effective (pregnancy rate is 25 per cent)
2. It should be clear that emergency contraception is not an abortifying medicine and not effective for the termination of pregnancy.
3. It may inhibit implantation but after the conception these are seldom effective.
4. Not effective to prevent sexually transmitted diseases.
5. The most common side effects are menstrual changes, fatigue, nausea, headache and abdominal pain.

Types of Emergency Pills

Emergency pills are of following types:

1. Standard Emergency Pills.
2. High dose oral contraceptive pills (daily pills i.e. COC and mini pills).

Standard Emergency Pills

Various brands of these pills are marketed under the label of emergency contraceptive pills. These pills are marketed in the pack of two tablets with each tablet containing 0.75 mg levonorgestrel. A first tablet (dose) is taken within 72 hours of unprotected sex and second tablets (dose) after 12 hours of first tablet.

Higher Dose of Oral Contraceptive Pills (Daily Pills i.e. COC and Mini Pills)

These are those pills which are routinely used as daily oral contraceptive pills. Depending upon the concentration of their hormonal contents, the number of tablets taken is different in first and second dose foe emergency contraception. A health practitioner can also plan the right dosage for emergency contraception by using different pills.

Emergency Contraceptives Pills (Levonergestril)

Sl. No.	Brand Name	Company	Rate (Rs.)
1.	I pills	Cipla	82
2.	Contra	Par labs	40
3.	ECEE2	German Remedies	35
4.	Unwanted 72	Mankind	50
5.	Pill 72	Cipla	34
6.	Norlevo	Win Medicare	45

Higher dose of Oral contraceptive pills (daily pills i.e. COC and mini pills)

Sl. No.	Composition	Brands	1st dose (within 72 hour)	2nd dose (after 12 hour of 1st dose)
1.	Low dose COC 0.15 or 0.25 mg Levonorgestel/ 0.5 mg norgestel (+) 0.03 mg ethinyl estradiol	Mala –D Bandhan Contra-L Cornil Femi Ovral-L	4 pills	4 pills
2.	Standard dose COC 0.15 or 0.25 mg Levonorgestel/ 0.5 mg norgestel (+) 0.05 mg ethinyl estradiol	Ovral Contra-P Regcyl Duoluton-L	2 pills	2 pills
3.	Progestin only pills 75 microgram of norgestrel	—	20 pills	20 pills
4.	Progestin only 30 microgram of levonorgestrel	—	25 pills	25 pills

(*For WHO Guidelines, see page no. 205*)

MT Pills

These pills are meant for termination of pregnancy or unwanted child i.e. abortion. MT pill is the last contraceptive weapon to get rid of the unwanted pregnancy. But it should be clear that self-medication may prove fatal sometimes.

It is advised to the committed couples that always choose a better method for their family planning. Method should be comfortable, easy to adopt, safe for longer duration and without any significant side effects. Committed and/or unmarried couples can also adopt barrier methods for the practice of safer sex and emergency contraceptive should be their last option. Usage of MT Pills should be last thing in the mind, albeit they do provide significant protection from unwanted pregnancy, and hence their role cannot be sidelined, even if they should be the last option.

Facts about MT Pills

- Sometimes may prove lethal if used without the supervision/prescription of a doctor.
- Adversely affects woman's health sometimes.
- Use as early as possible after the confirmation of pregnancy.
- Effective up to 7 weeks of conception but usually not recommended after 4 weeks.
- Consult immediately with the physician if there is prolonged and severe heavy bleeding.
- Ultrasound of uterus is always recommended for the proper clearance of fetal parts.
- Some patients need surgical curettage especially unmarried woman due to the tight internal os.
- If this method fails, a surgical abortion would be required.
- Other side effects include cramping, diarrhea, nausea, vomiting, and headache.

Action Mechanism of MT Pills

One MT pill pack contains two types of tablets or drugs and systematic use of both drugs is effective for abortion.

1st Dose (Mifepristone)

- It is taken orally and work against pregnancy hormone (progesterone) which is critical to maintain the pregnancy.
- It helps in the detachment of zygote from uterine wall.

2nd Dose (Misoprostol)

- Second pill is taken through the oral or vaginal route (inserted into deep into the vagina).
- Pills inserted vaginally are more effective.
- Use within 3 days or between 24 to 72 hours only
- Causes extreme spasm in the smooth muscle of uterine cavity.
- These vigorous contractions helps to expel the detached embryo and other aborted fetal tissue remains in the womb.
- The patient aborts spontaneously after 3-5 hours after taking the second dose (by vaginal route).
- There have been no complications though bleeding may occur and it may continue for 3-7 days.

1st dose recommended usually contains 600 mg of mifepristone (3 tablets, each tablet containing 200 mg of mifepristone) and 2nd dose contains 400 mcg of misoprostol (2 tablets, each tablet containing 200 mcg of misoprostol) i.e. 3 + 2 regimen. Due to the cost of the medicine some doctors also use 1 + 3 regimen during early pregnancy.

As previously described, continuous vaginal bleeding is also reported that may be very intense and uncontrollable. In this case immediate hospitalization is required to avoid any further mishappening.

9

Medical Termination of Pregnancy (MTP) (Abortion)

Abortion refers to the termination of pregnancy before 20 weeks of gestation (within 20 week from the onset of last menses). It is of two types:

- Early Abortion: before 12 weeks
- Late Abortion: from 12-20 weeks

Types of Abortions: On the basis of nature, abortions are of following eight types:

1. Spontaneous Abortion

Occurs naturally, without any apparent cause and is also known by the name of miscarriage. When there is the spontaneous loss of a fetus before the 20th week of pregnancy, the aborted fetus is incapable of surviving.

Genetic anomalies (problems) in the fetus are the major cause of miscarriage. Mothers suffering from diabetes, thyroid problems, hormonal factors, infections and certain other factors also suffers spontaneous abortions.

In confirmed pregnancies, the incidence of spontaneous abortion is around 10 to 15 per cent. Incidence is probably higher because some very early abortions are mistaken for a late menstrual period.

2. Recurrent Abortion or Habitual Abortion

Three or more consecutive spontaneous abortions that occur at about the same stage of pregnancy, are known as recurrent abortions.

One sporadic abortion generally does not increase the risk of repeated abortions, but there are certain factors that are directly associated with the recurrent abortions i.e.

- Genetic defects (chromosomal abnormality) in the fetus or in anyone or both the partners.
- Hormonal problems (progesterone deficiency or luteal phase defects, polycystic ovary disease).
- Woman suffering from thyroid abnormalities or diabetes.
- Cervical incompetence and infections.
- Uterine defects.
- Effects of certain chemicals, X-rays, and other noxious agents.
- Psychological factors.
- Some other typical medical problems (diseases) which can be diagnosed by doctors.

3. Missed Abortion

In this case fetus is retained for several weeks, but it no longer develops normally, no uterine growth or regression or loss of weight is observed in the pregnancy.

4. Inevitable Abortion

Inevitable abortion is a spontaneous abortion which cannot be stopped. Symptoms include lower abdominal cramping and bleeding. The uterine cervix is dilated and fetal or placental material may already have passed out of the body.

Inevitable abortion is defined as bleeding of intrauterine origin with continuous and progressive dilation of the cervix but without expulsion of conception products before the 20th week of gestation.

An *inevitable abortion* describes the conditions or stage where the fetal heart beat is shown to have stopped and the cervix has already dilated open, but the fetus has yet to be expelled.

5. Threatened Abortion

A threatened abortion is a condition that suggests a miscarriage might take place before the 20th week of pregnancy. Bleeding occurs during early pregnancy. Prognosis is worse when pain and cramping are experienced.

6. Blighted Ovum Abortion

A blighted ovum is characterized through ultrasound as anembryonic pregnancy (absence of an embryo in the womb). In this case a fertilized egg implants in the uterus but the resulting embryo either stops developing very early or doesn't form at all.

It may also be a common reason for the spontaneous abortion in initial stage. Due to an early pregnancy loss, women get a positive result on a pregnancy test, because the placenta begins to develop. Some symptoms which are common in a normal pregnancy, such as fatigue, nausea, and sore breasts are also observed but few days later woman becomes normal.

But if the pregnancy is not terminated spontaneously, woman needs some medication to speed up this procedure or need other procedures like D & C.

7. Therapeutic Abortion

It is defined as the termination of pregnancy before the reaching of fetal viability, in order to preserve maternal physical or mental health. Therapeutic abortion can be performed to:

- Save the life of the mother,
- Preserve the health of the mother,
- Abort genetically abnormal child
- Terminate a nonviable pregnancy,
- Electively reduce a multi-fetal pregnancy.

8. Elective/Induced Abortion

Voluntary interruption of pregnancy between the implantation and age of viability. This is very common and a woman chooses to end a pregnancy before the child is ready to be born, due to following reasons:

- Unwanted or unplanned pregnancy.
- Abortion for proper spacing of children.
- Unable to rear the child.
- Pregnancy of unmarried woman or girls.

METHODS OF ABORTION (TERMINATION OF PREGNANCY)

1. First Trimester Termination: Upto 12 weeks.
2. Mid-Trimester or Second Trimester Abortion: 12-20 weeks.

1. First Trimester Termination: Upto 12 Weeks

A. Medical Abortion.

B. Early Uterine Evacuation (EUE), Minisuction, Menstrual Regulation.

C. Surgical methods of 1st trimester

   I. Suction Evacuation/Suction Aspiration/ Vacuum Aspiration.

   II. Suction Curettage.

   III. Dilation and Curettage (D & C).

A. Medical Abortion

Mentioned in the previous chapter (Emergency and MT Pills).

B. Early Uterine Evacuation (EUE) or Minisuction or Menstrual Regulation

Also known by the name of mini abortion or lunch time abortion as it hardly take 10 minutes to complete. It is best for 1 to 3 weeks of pregnancy, from the date of onset of last menses.

In this case a woman has no need for hospitalization. A thin plastic tube is inserted into the uterus and its contents sucked out by negative pressure created in a syringe (menstruation regulation syringe).

Advantages of Mini-abortion

1. In this procedure surgical risks are very few.
2. Can be performed without any help of anesthesia.
3. The person can go to home early and resume her normal activities.

Disadvantages of Mini-abortion

1. There are some chances of failure of this procedure.
2. Infection can take place.
3. Bleeding may occur.

C. Surgical Methods of 1st Trimester Abortion

It is also not more than 15 minutes procedure. Abortion through these methods is usually done in the early pregnancy, i.e. before 12 weeks, through following steps:

The lady is made to lie on her back with her legs raised and placed in the stirrups.

Using the local anesthesia, dilating the cervix, with the help of dilator and introducing hollow metal rods of increasing diameters and then evacuating the contents of the uterus mechanically by scraping or by suction or both.

Surgical methods of 1st trimester abortion which are generally used are:

I. Suction Evacuation/Suction Aspiration/Vacuum Aspiration: A surgical procedure in which the cervix is dilated (opened) and vacuum is used to remove tissue from the uterus.

II. Suction Curettage: This is the most common method of abortion during the first 12 weeks of the pregnancy in which the contents of the uterus are withdrawn through a narrow tube called as suction curettage/vacuum curettage. This is also a very short duration procedure having following steps:

1. A suction curette (hollow tube with a knife-edge tip) is inserted into the womb.

2. Suction curette is connected to a vacuum machine by a transparent tube.
3. The vacuum suction is more powerful that tears the embryo into pieces which are then sucked out through the tube into a bottle.

III. Dilatation and Curettage (D & C)**:** It is very similar to the suction method with the additional insertion of a loop-shaped knife (manually as well as with the help of an instrument) which cuts the fetus into short pieces. These pieces are scraped out through the cervix.

This method is also used for some other therapeutic purposes, other than the pregnancy.

Advantages of Surgical method of 1st trimester abortion

1. Very simple and safe procedures involving few steps.

The person can go home and resume her normal activities soon.

Blood loss is minimal.

Most effective with least failure rate.

After this procedure woman have a choice to insert any IUD for further protection.

Disadvantages of Surgical methods of 1st trimester abortion

1. Side effects of anesthesia may be observed.
2. Damage in the cervix and uterus may also be observed
3. Infection of the uterus and fallopian tubes is also a common problem if precautions were not taken properly.
4. Bleeding may be observed.
5. The method is not suitable for bigger sized uterus of > 10 weeks as chances of retained products are more.

2. Mid-Trimester or Second Trimester Abortion

A. Dilatation and evacuation (D & E)

B. Intrauterine injection of abortifacients

C. Prostaglandin vaginal suppositories

D. Hysterotomy

A. Dilatation and Evacuation (D & E)

This procedure is generally used after 12 weeks upto 18 weeks (LMP) of gestation. This is a two step procedure; initially the cervix is dilated, followed by the evacuation of uterine cavity.

Dilatation: This is of following two types:

I. Rapid Method

II. Slow Method

I. Rapid Method: The cervix is properly dilated (opened) due to comparatively large size of fetus. Sometimes local anesthesia (paracervical block), sedative (diazepam) or painkillers are also used by the doctor to reduce the pain experienced by a woman.

Cervix is dilated with the cervical dilators.

Drawbacks

- Chance of cervical injury is more
- Not suitable, if fetus > 8 weeks.

II. Slow Method: Some hygroscopic agents like Laminaria Tents, Isoptent (made from Isapgol husk) and some synthetic hydrogels (i.e. Lemical, hypan, Dilapan, etc.), act by radial force, extracting water from stroma and swell without lengthening, resulting in gradual, atraumatic and reversible dilation of cervix.

Advantages

- Chance of cervical injury is minimal.

Disadvantages

- Hospitalization for one day.
- More chances of sepsis.

Evacuation: In the place of the curette used in D&C abortions, a pair of forceps is inserted into the womb to grasp a part of the fetus. The teeth of the forceps twist and tear the calcified bones and other parts of the fetus. Comparatively large size of fetus, the process is repeated until the whole fetus is totally dismembered and removed out.

B. Inter/Intrauterine Injection of Abortifacient

Abortifacient are the agents which induces the abortion. Some prostaglandins, hypertonic saline, hypertonic urea, are introduced into the amniotic fluid (fluid surrounding the baby). Another method is the Installation of 0.1 per cent ethacridine lactate in extra amniotic membranes. Fetus and placenta are aborted vaginally

Salt Poisoning (Saline Injection): Injections of strong salt solution (20 per cent saline) directly into the amniotic sac (fluid surrounding the baby) kills the fetus within an hour and the woman delivers the dead baby in a day or two.

A needle is inserted through the abdominal wall, then through the uterine wall and into the amniotic sac. During the process amniotic fluid is replaced with a concentrated salt solution. Amount of saline required is calculated- as follows

Number of weeks of gestation × 10 ml.

It is quite risky for a woman.

Urea Abortion Method: The procedure is similar to the salt poisoning; instead of 20 per cent saline solution, 40 per cent urea solution is injected into the amniotic sac. Both methods involve following precautions:

A. Be sure that the needle is in the amniotic cavity evidenced by the flow of the clear amniotic liquor/fluid.

B. Careful monitoring.

C. If symptoms like, acute abdominal pain, headache, thrust appears—stop the injection (abortifacient) and give a rapid infusion of 1000 ml of dextrose in water along with intra-venous (I/V) diuretics. (The agents which causes increased urine outflow).

Routine antibiotic: Ampilllcin/500 mg TDS × 3-5 days are also given.

Osmotic dilators are used to decrease the time to delivery and decrease complications.

Inter-uterine Injection (Extra Amniotic Injection): Installation of 0.1 per cent ethacridine lactate (10 ml/week of gestation) used in those cases where the saline and urea not tolerated. Given trancervically by a Foley's Catheter (No. 16). The catheter is passed upto the cervical canal to about 10 cm above the internal os between membranes and myometrium. It is removed after 4 hours and after 20 to 40 hours; 'mini labor' ensues/starts.

C. Prostaglandin Vaginal Suppositories

Contraceptive prostaglandins (i.e. PGE2, F2-alpha etc.) initiate strong contractions of the uterine smooth muscles by stimulating myometrium and promote cervical softening, effacement, and dilation. These are also available in another form like endocervical gel or vaginal insert.

20 mg suppositories of PGE2 are typically given for 3-5 hours and are not to exceed total a dosage of 240 mg or duration of 48 hours.

PGF2 alpha (PGF2α) - 250 mg intra-muscularly IM for 2 hours is also available but these prostaglandins should be used under the strict guidance of the doctors.

D. Hysterotomy Abortion

It is last option of termination of pregnancy when all above mentioned methods could not be employed or they have failed. Operative procedure is quite similar to the caesarean operation in which the uterus is opened through an abdominal incision and the fetus is removed, albeit, incision is comparatively shorter. It is used between the 12th and 20th week of pregnancy.

Possible Complications and Risks of Abortion

1. Immediate Complication

A. Complications of Local Anesthesia: These are very rare but sometimes needle (containing anesthetic or sedative drug) may be wrongly injected into the blood vessels. As a result breathing may become rapid, drowsiness, vertigo, blurred vision, vomiting, diarrhea, and convulsion may be reported.

B. Allergic Reaction or Hypersensitivity: Some common allergic reactions, occurs immediately or after few hours like the swelling of the eyelids, bronchospasm, joint pains, urticaria etc. Injection of Avil, Phenargan (25 mg), Efcorlin (100mg), dexamethosone (4 mg) etc. are quite effective to treat them.

2. Complication during Procedure

1. Very rarely scratches, cuts or torn on the cervix may occur. This happen when the cervix is not sufficiently soft, or in case of the forcible rapid mechanical dilatation beyond 10mm and or when there is difficulty in dilating.
2. Some times perforation of the uterus may occur, especially in the following cases:
    - Repeated abortions.
    - Uterus is not in its normal position (retroverted or anteverted).
    - Previous uterine surgery or caesarian operation.
3. Incomplete emptying of the uterus-fetal tissue left inside the uterus, for which repeated vacuum aspiration may be necessary.
4. Heavy bleeding -very rarely-a hemorrhage develops; medication, repeated vacuum aspiration, surgery or blood transfusion might be needed.

3. Post -treatment Complications

1. Infection is a common problem, sterilized instrument should be used and take proper antibiotics after the procedure or in rare cases, repeated vacuum aspiration might be needed.

2. Fertility can be diminished due to following reasons:
    - Cervical injury—Can cause cervical incompetence (in which the baby could not be held inside the womb) which is the common cause of pre-term birth and mid-term, second trimester pregnancy loss.
    - Secondary Amenorrhea—Also cause infertility, this may be due excessive and vigorous curettage.
    - Chronic Pelvic Inflammation—After MTP, this complication may cause ectopic pregnancy, menstrual disorders or secondary infertility.
    - Conception problems due to the adherent placenta.

10

Medical Termination of Pregnancy Act

THE MEDICAL TERMINATION OF PREGNANCY ACT, 1971 (ACT NO. 34 OF 1971)

(10th August 1971)

An Act to provide for the termination of certain pregnancies by registered Medical Practitioners and for matters connected therewith or incidental thereto.

Be it enacted by Parliament in the Twenty-second Year of the Republic of India as follows:

1. Short title, extent and commencement

(1) This Act may be called the Medical Termination of Pregnancy Act, 1971.

(2) It extends to the whole of India except the State of Jammu and Kashmir.

(3) It shall come into force on such date as the Central Government may, by notification in the Official Gazette, appoint.

2. Definitions — In this Act, unless the context otherwise requires

(a) "guardian" means a person having the care of the person of a minor or a lunatic;

(b) "lunatic" has the meaning assigned to it in section 3 of the Indian Lunatic Act, 1912 (4 of 1912);

(c) "minor" means a person who, under the provisions of the Indian Majority Act, 1875 (9 of 1875), is to be deemed not to have attained his majority;

(d) "registered medical practitioner" means a medical practitioner who possesses any recognized medical qualification as defined in clause (h) of section 2 of the Indian Medical Council Act, 1956 (102 of 1956), whose name has been entered in a State Medical Register and who has such experience or training in gynaecology and obstetrics as may be prescribed by rules made under this Act.

3. When pregnancies may be terminated by registered medical practitioners

(1) Notwithstanding anything contained in the Indian Penal Code (45 of 1860), a registered medical practitioner shall not be guilty of any offence under that Code or under any other law for the time being in force, if any pregnancy is terminated by him in accordance with the provisions of this Act.

(2) Subject to the provisions of sub-section (4), a pregnancy may be terminated by a registered medical practitioner,

(a) Where the length of the pregnancy does not exceed twelve weeks if such medical practitioner is, or

(b) Where the length of the pregnancy exceeds twelve weeks but does not exceed twenty weeks, if not less than two registered medical practitioners are, of opinion, formed in good faith, that

(i) the continuance of the pregnancy would involve a risk to the life of the pregnant woman or of grave injury to her physical or mental health; or

(ii) there is a substantial risk that if the child were born, it would suffer from such physical or mental abnormalities to be seriously handicapped.

Explanation 1. Where any pregnancy is alleged by the pregnant woman to have been caused by rape, the anguish caused by such pregnancy shall be presumed to constitute a grave injury to the mental health of the pregnant woman.

Explanation 2. Where any pregnancy occurs as a result of failure of any device or method used by any married woman or her husband for the purpose of limiting the number of children, the anguish caused by such unwanted pregnancy may be resumed to constitute a grave injury to the mental health of the pregnant woman.

(3) In determining whether the continuance of a pregnancy would involve such risk of injury to the health as is mentioned in sub-section (2), account may be taken of the pregnant women's actual or reasonable foreseeable environment.

(4) (a) No pregnancy of a woman, who has not attained the age of eighteen years, or, who, having attained the age of eighteen years, is a lunatic, shall be terminated except with the consent in writing of her guardian.

(b) Save as otherwise provided in clause (a), no pregnancy shall be terminated except with the consent of the pregnant woman.

4. Place where pregnancy may be terminated

No Termination of pregnancy shall be made in accordance with this Act at any place other than:

(a) a hospital established or maintained by Government, or

(b) a place for the time being approved for the purpose of this Act by Government.

5. Sections 3 and 4 when not to apply

(1) The provisions of section 4, and so much of the provisions of sub-section (2) of section 3 as relate to

the length of the pregnancy and the opinion of not less than two registered medical practitioners, shall not apply to the termination of a pregnancy by a registered medical practitioner in a case where he is of opinion, formed in good faith, that the termination of such pregnancy is immediately necessary to save the life of the pregnant woman.

(2) Notwithstanding anything contained in the Indian Penal Code (45 of 1860), the termination of a pregnancy by a person who is not a registered medical practitioner shall be an offence punishable under that Code, and that Code shall, to this extent, stand modified.

Explanation. For the purposes of this section, so much of the provisions of clause (d) of section (2) as relate to the possession, by a registered medical practitioner, of experience or training in gynaecology and obstetrics shall not apply.

6. Power to make rules

(1) The Central Government may, by notification in the Official Gazette, make rules to carry out the provisions of this Act.

(2) In particular, and without prejudice to the generality of the foregoing power, such rules may provide for all or any of the following matters, namely:

(a) the experience or training, or both, which is registered medical practitioner shall have if he intends to terminate any pregnancy under this Act; and

(b) Such other matters as are required to be or may be, provided by rules made under this Act.

(3) Every rule made by the Central Government under this Act shall be laid, as soon as may be after it is made, before each House of Parliament while it is in session for a total period of thirty days which may be comprised in one session or in two successive sessions,

and if, before the expiry of the session in which it is so laid or the session immediately following, both Houses agree in making any modification in the rule or both Houses agree that the rule should not be made, the rule shall thereafter have effect only in such modified form or be of no effect, as the case may be; so, however, that any such modification or annulment shall be without prejudice to the validity of anything previously done under that rule.

7. Power to make regulations

(1) The State Government may, by regulations:

(a) require any such opinion as is referred to in sub-section (2) of section 3 to be certified by a registered medical practitioner or practitioners concerned, in such form and at such time as may be specified in such regulations, and the preservation or disposal of such certificates;

(b) require any registered medical practitioner, who terminates a pregnancy, to give intimation of such termination and such other information relating to the termination as may be specified in such regulations;

(c) prohibit the disclosure, except to such purposes as may be specified in such regulations, of intimations given or information furnished in pursuance of such regulations.

(2) The intimation given and the information furnished in pursuance of regulations made by virtue of clause (b) of sub-section (1) shall be given or furnished, as the case may be, to the Chief Medical Officer of the State.

(3) Any person who will fully contravenes or willfully fails to comply with the requirements of any regulation made under sub-section (1) shall be liable to be punished with fine, which may extend to one thousand rupees.

8. Protection of action taken in good faith

No suit or legal proceedings shall lie against any registered medical practitioner for any damage caused or likely to be caused by anything, which is in good faith done or intended to be done under this Act.

THE MEDICAL TERMINATION OF PREGNANCY AMENDMENT ACT, 2002 (NO. 64 OF 2002) (18th December 2002)

An Act to amend the Medical Termination of Pregnancy Act, 1971.

Be it enacted by Parliament in the Fifty-third Year of the Republic of India as follows:

(1) This Act may be called the Medical Termination of Pregnancy (Amendment) Act, 2002.

(2) It shall come into force on such date as the Central Government may, by notification in the Official Gazette, appoint.

In section 2 of the Medical Termination of Pregnancy Act, 34 of 1971, (hereinafter referred to as the principal Act),

(i) in clause (a), for the word "lunatic", the words 'mentally ill person" shall be substituted.

(ii) For clause (b), the following clause shall be substituted, namely:

'(b) "mentally ill person" means a person who is in need of treatment by reason of any mental disorder other than mental retardation;'.

(3) In section 3 of the principal Act, in sub-section (4), in clause (a), for the word "lunatic", the words "mentally ill person" shall be substituted.

4. For section 4 of the principal Act, the following section shall be substituted, namely:

"4. No termination of pregnancy shall be made in accordance with this Act at any place other than:

(a) a hospital established or maintained by Government, or

(b) a place for the time being approved for the purpose of this Act by Government or a District Level Committee constituted by that Government with the Chief Medical Officer or District Health Officer as the Chairperson of the said Committee:
Provided that the District Level Committee shall consist of not less than three and not more than five members including the Chairperson, as the Government may specify from time to time:"

5. In section 5 of the principal Act, for sub-section (2) and the Explanation thereto, the following shall be substituted, namely:

(1) Notwithstanding anything contained in the Indian Penal Code, the termination of pregnancy by a person who is not a registered medical practitioner shall be an offence punishable with rigorous imprisonment for a term which shall not be less than two years but which may extend to seven years under that Code, and that Code shall, to this extent, stand modified.

(2) Whoever terminates any pregnancy in a place other than that mentioned in section 4, shall be punishable with rigorous imprisonment for a term which shall not be less than two years but which may extend to seven years.

(3) Any person being owner of a place which is not approved under clause (b) of section 4 shall be punishable with rigorous imprisonment for a term which shall not be less than two years but which may extend to seven years.

Explanation 1

For the purposes of this section, the expression "owner" in relation to a place means any person who is the administrative head or otherwise responsible for the working or maintenance of a hospital or place, by whatever name called, where the pregnancy may be terminated under this Act.

Explanation 2

For the purposes of this section, so much of the provisions of clause (d) of section 2 as relate to the possession, by registered medical practitioner, of experience or training in gynaecology and obstetrics shall not apply.

Highlights of Medical Termination Of Pregnancy Act (MTP ACT)

In India, MTP act was passed in 1971. This act legalizes abortion on following grounds:

Medical Grounds

Where the continuation of pregnancy would involve serious risk of life or grave injury to the physical and mental health of the pregnant women. For example, Severe Cardiac Diseases, TB, Malignant Weight, DM, Epilepsy, malignancy (cancer), etc.

Eugenic Grounds

Where there is a substantial risk of the child being born with serious physical and mental abnormalities and is not expected to have a good quality of life.

Humanitarian Grounds

When the pregnancy is caused by rape, etc.

Social Grounds

1. Pregnancy caused as a result of the failure of contraceptive.
2. Poor socio-economic status, etc.
3. Single mothers.

Recommendations

1. Only that RMP is qualified to perform an MTP provided:
   - One has assisted in at least 25 MTP in an authorized centre and is having a certificate.
   - One has got 6 months house surgeon training on obstetrics and gynaecology.
   - One have diploma or degree in obstetrics and gynaecology.
2. Pregnancy termination can be done in an authorized centre only.
3. Written consent of women is must. Husband's consent is not required.
4. Termination of pregnancy in a minor girl (< 18 yrs) or mentally ill, requires the consent of parents or legal guardians.
5. Termination is permitted up to 20 weeks of pregnancy.
   - If duration < 12 weeks, consent of one medical practitioner
   - If duration > 12 weeks, consents of 2 medical practitioners is mandatory.

The abortion has to be performed confidentially and is to be reported to the DGHS (Director General, Health Services) of state.

Source: www. mohfw.nic.in
www. health.nic.in

Family Planning

1. Tubectomy
2. Vasectomy
3. Family Planning and Family Planning Programme
4. Family Planning Insurance Scheme

1

Tubectomy

This is the process in which a female permanently rids herself of the burden of any unwanted conception. In India, females prefer this method after having two or more children as compared to other hormonal/nonhormonal methods. It is frequently chosen by women who do not want any more children, but who are still sexually active and potentially fertile, and want to be free of the limitations of other types of birth control measure.

This is a surgical procedure and performed by a specially trained surgeon. Many Govt. agencies promote this procedure by providing financial aid to the patients and all the operation charges are free. The process of ending a woman's ability to conceive by tying off or cutting a part the Fallopian tubes, forms the basis of this method, though these days, reversible methods are preferred, so that a woman can opt to regain fertility, if she feels the need for it.

Benefit of Tubectomy

- Permanently free from the burden of conception.
- Free from side effects of other hormonal contraceptives.
- Performed by trained surgeon. Private clinics empanelled with government also do the same for free (private clinician receives an amount of Rs. 1300 from the Govt.).

- Woman working for Govt. and other sister concerns, get a 6 weeks paid leave for tubectomy and two weeks immediately following the day of an tubectomy.
- A woman suffering from illness arising from tubectomy operation will be entitled, in addition to the period of absence allowed to her, leave with wage at the rate of maternity benefit for a maximum period of one month.
- Earlier, all women going in for a tubectomy got a monetary incentive. Now only the SC/ST women would get Rs. 150 as the incentive.
- Security from Govt. for any further conception and related problems is provided.

Procedure

In this method a woman's fallopian tubes are surgically cut or blocked off to prevent the union of the egg and sperm (fertilization), the basis of conception. These tubes, which are about 10 cm long and 0.5 cm in diameter, are found on the upper outer sides of the uterus, and open into the uterus through small channels.

It is a very simple procedure and takes 15 to 20 minute and is performed under general anesthesia, or local anesthesia or spinal anesthesia, with sedation. These days, this is done through laparoscopy and mini-laparotomy. In a laparoscopic tubal ligation, a long, thin telescope like surgical instrument called a laparoscope is inserted into the pelvis through a small cut about 1 cm long near the navel. Carbon dioxide gas is pumped in to help move the abdominal wall to give the surgeon easier access to the tubes. Often the surgical instruments are inserted through a second incision near the pubic-hair line. An instrument may be placed through the vagina to hold the uterus in place.

In a mini-laparotomy, a 3-4 cm incision is made just above the pubic bone or under the navel. A larger incision, or laparotomy, is rarely used today. Tubal ligation can also be performed at the time of a cesarean operation/section.

Before Operation Following Points should be Kept in Mind:

- Educate and counsel the patient.
- Awareness about the risks of anesthesia and surgery.
- Tubectomy should ideally be done within a week after menstruation.
- Refrain from sexual intercourse for at least 4 days before tubectomy. If having sexual intercourse, use a condom to avoid the risk of ectopic/normal pregnancy.
- Properly review the medical history, physical examination and laboratory testing are must before the procedure.

After Operation Following Points should be Kept in Mind:

- After operation, patient should be monitored for several hours before discharge from the clinic.
- Recommend proper bed rest for few days and avoidance of any heavy work till the healing of the wound.
- Possible side effects includes infection and bleeding, if seen, immediately contact a doctor.
- To carefully monitor other signs such as fever, nausea, vomiting, drowsiness, or pain, these could be indicating that complications have occurred.
- Recovery period is very short, around 3-4 days, after that when the patient feels better, sexual activity can be resumed.

Which is the Better Method?

Generally tubectomy is done with 1) Laparoscopy and with (2) Mini laparotomy. Operation through laparoscopy is better than mini-laparotomy because it causes very little pain, bleeding, infections and other problems but the patient may experience pain in the shoulder area from the carbon dioxide used during surgery. Recovery period is also very short with laparoscopy methods.

(*For WHO Guidelines, see page no. 206*)

2
Vasectomy

Males have only two methods for birth control i.e. using condom and vasectomy available to them. As compared to condom, vasectomy, is permanent method of birth control involving a minor surgical operation. This is the best present of the husbands who loves their wives a lot.

During the vasectomy, the vas deferens that carries the sperm from testicles to the ejaculatory duct or penis is clamped, cut, or otherwise sealed. Vasectomy blocks only sperm transportation and not the semen ejaculation from the male partner to the female partner.

Normal man-semen contains sperms
Vasectomised person-semen is without sperms

In vasectomy — testis is working properly, sperms and sex hormones are properly produced and only transportation of sperms is blocked.

Some Rumors about the Vasectomy

Rumor No. 1: Vasectomy is similar to castration: castration is the process of removing and/or inhibiting the development and function of testes.

Rumor No. 2: Vasectomy has significant effect on the following:

1. Sexual performance and masculinity
2. Decreases sexual desire

3. Causes impotence
4. Prevents orgasm
5. Reduces sexual pleasure
6. Causes a man's voice to sound like a woman's

All above mentioned characters are controlled by sex hormones and vasectomised persons have similar hormone production (vasectomy does not inhibit the function of the testes).

Rumor No. 3: Shrinks the testicles and hinders the ejaculation:

This is not true; testes receive proper blood supply for their functioning, hormones are properly produced and circulated and they maintain the functions of other sexual organs.

Rumor No. 4: These are the following blind rumors:

It causes weakness and severe pains in various body parts, backaches, weight gain, baldness, poor vision and other psychiatric disorders. These are false.

Advantages

1. It is very effective and is a permanent method.
2. Burden free sexual life as well as freedom from the side effects of the hormonal contraceptives for the wife.
3. No apparent long-term health risks.

Disadvantages

1. It is permanent method, so think well and consult with wife properly before undergoing the process.
2. There are some common complications of surgery like brief drowsiness and feeling little uncomfortable for 2 to 3 days.
3. Not effective immediately, as few sperms remains in the vas and are ejaculated in the semen for some days after vasectomy.
4. Bleeding, infections and some other complications may also be observed in few patients.

5. Always recommend to the patient the use of condom during sexual intercourse for up to 30 times or use any other contraceptive for at least 3 months, after vasectomy.

Procedure of Operation

Operation is very simple and takes not more than 30 minutes to complete. To make the patients relaxed and sleepy, some anesthetic drugs are given through oral or IV (intravenous) routes. Testes are cleaned properly with an antiseptic, vas is located, and some local anesthesia may also be applied into surrounding area. Surgeon makes a cut or a small opening into the scrotum and through this opening the two vas deferens tubes are cut and tied, stitched, or sealed at the cut ends of the vas deferens.

(*For WHO Guidelines, see page no. 207*)

3

Family Planning and Family Planning Programme

The family planning is a planning by the couple to regulate the number and spacing of their children through the practice of contraception or other methods of birth control. It is surprising that in India around 75 per cent of the pregnancies are unplanned and out of them 25 per cent are unwanted and these unwanted children are more likely to die as compared to the planned pregnancy. Majority of these unplanned pregnancies leads to short birth interval between the two successive children, which is the major cause of malnutrition and child death. High fertility rate due to unplanned and unwanted pregnancy adversely affects the health and life of a female Knowledge of family planning should be compulsory for every individual who is going for marriage. Family planning not only improves the quality of life but also the economic power significantly. Children get more attention and better educational opportunities in the society.

Salient Benefits of Family Planning

- Equal emphasis on both spacing and limiting methods.

- Pregnancy and Children by choice and not by chance.
- More facility as well opportunity to their children.

India was the first country in the world which formulated a national family planning programme in 1952. Data from the family planning in 2000 reported that among married women, 48 per cent use various types of contraception for spacing and limiting the child birth. In 48 per cent women, 34 per cent are those who rely upon female sterilization, 5.5 per cent on traditional and natural methods and 2 per cent on male sterilization. It's really a matter of great debate why more than half of the married women are not using any birth spacing/ contraceptives method and why only less than 7 per cent women rely upon pills, condom and IUDs.

Following factors are to be blamed to some extents; one quarter of India's population currently lives below the national poverty line, 72 per cent population resides in rural and other interior regions, 80 per cent of the entire population survives on less than Rs. 100 per day, illiteracy and unawareness. These are the major ones that may affect the family planning programme and policies. Inadequate knowledge of contraceptive methods and incomplete or erroneous information about where to obtain these methods, and aids how to use them are the main reasons cited for the low acceptance of the family planning. We cannot ignore the role of the Indian Govt. in the proper implementation of family planning programme.

With a view to encourage people to adopt birth control and permanent method of Family Planning, Government has been implementing centrally sponsored schemes from time to time. After reviewing the various family planning programmes, authorities of family planning are highly concerned regarding the following issues:

1. Addressing the unmet need in contraception through:
   - Assured delivery of family planning services.
   - Developing skilled manpower for the same.
2. Increasing basket of choices

3. Promoting contraception through increased advocacy.
4. Increasing male participation through intensive promotion of Non Scalpel Vasectomy (NSP).
5. Promotion of IUDs as a short and long-term spacing method.
6. Promotion of emergency contraceptive pills.
7. Ensuring quality care in Family Planning Services.
8. Promoting Public Private Partnerships (PPP).
9. Revised compensation scheme.
10. Family planning insurance scheme.

Ministry of health and family welfare encourages people to adopt permanent methods of Family Planning and it provides cash compensation to the acceptors of sterilization and compensates the loss of wages for the day on which he/she attended the medical facility for undergoing sterilization. Government has been implementing a Centrally Sponsored Scheme since 1981 to compensate for the loss of wages to the acceptors of sterilization services and also revised the compensatory amount from time to time.

Highlights and Overview of the Revised Compensation Scheme

Recently, on 29th October, 2007 Ministry of Health and Family Welfare revised compensation package to the acceptor of sterilization and IUD insertion at public as well as private accredited health facilities, and formed new guidelines for the sterilization at the accredited private centre/NGO in non high and high focus states (NHFS and HFS) and for the sterilization done at Govt. institutions by empanelled private doctors.

Revised Compensation (in Rs.) in High Focus States

***High focus 18 States:** Bihar, Uttar Pradesh (UP), Madhya Pradesh (MP), Rajasthan, Jharkhand, Chatisgarh, Uttrakhand, Orissa, Jammu-Kashmir, Himachal Pradesh, Assam, Arunachal Pradesh, Manipur, Mizoram, Meghalya, Nagaland, Tripura, Sikkim

1. Availing Public Facilities for Sterilization

Breakage of the Compensation package	Acceptor	Motivator	Drugs and dressing	Surgeon Charge	Anesthetic charges	Staff Nurse	OT Technician	Refreshment	Camp management	Total
Vasectomy (ALL)	1100	200	50	100	-	15	15	10	10	1500
Tubectomy (ALL)	600	150	100	75	25	15	15	10	10	1000

2. Availing Private Facilities for Sterilization

Category	Type of operation	Facility	Motivator	Total
* High focus 18 States	Vasectomy (ALL) Tubectomy (ALL)	1300 1350	200 150	1500 1500

Revised Compensation in Non-High Focus States

****Non-High focus 17 States/UTs:** Karnataka, Kerala, Tamil Nadu (TN), Andhra Pradesh (AP), Maharashtra, Goa, Gujarat, Punjab, Haryana, West Bengal (WB), Delhi, Chandigarh, Puducherry, Andaman & Nicobar Islands, Lakshadweep & Minicoy Islands, Dadra & Nagar Haveli, Daman & Diu.

1. Availing Public Facilities for Sterilization

Breakage of the Compensation package	Acceptor	Motivator	Drugs and dressing	Surgeon charge	Anesthetic charges	Staff Nurse	OT Technician	Refresh-ment	Camp management	Total
Vasec-tomy(ALL)	1100	200	50	100	-	15	15	10	10	1500
Tubec-tomy (BPL+SC/ST only)	600	150	100	75	25	15	15	10	10	1000
Tubectomy (APL only)	250	150	100	75	25	15	15	10	10	

2. Availing Private Facilities for Sterilization

Category	Type of operation	Facility	Motivator	Total
**Non High focus 17 States/UTs	Vasectomy (ALL) Tubectomy (ALL)	1300 1350	200 150	1500 1500

The general guidelines and salient features of the new revised scheme are as follows:

1. Extension of the increased package for vasectomy to all categories in all states including APL (above poverty lines) of non high focus states both for public and accredited private/NGO facilities.
2. Extension of the increased package for tubectomy to all categories in High Focus States and to BPL/SC/ST only in Non High Focus States in the public sector.
3. Enhancement of the existing scheme for APL client of tubectomy of Non High Focus States from Rs. 300 to Rs. 650 in the public facilities in line with the increase to the motivators and service providers for BPL/SC/ST categories to ensure that they don't discriminate between different categories of clients and provides the best possible service to all clients.
4. Extension of the increased package for tubectomy to all categories in the High Focus States and BPL/SC/ST only in the Non High Focus states in the accredited private/NGO sector.
5. No compensation scheme is admissible to APL client for tubectomy in the Non High Focus states in the accredited private/NGO facilities.
6. Increasing the Compensation Package from existing Rs. 800 to Rs. 1500 for vasectomy in public facilities.
7. Increasing the Compensation Package from existing Rs. 800 to Rs. 1000 for tubectomy in public facilities.
8. Out of the compensation package of Rs. 1500 for vasectomy, an amount of Rs. 1100 and out of the package of Rs. 1000 for tubectomy, an amount of Rs. 600 is to be paid to an acceptor as compensation for loss of wages.
9. No compensation is payable to the acceptors if he or she opts to avail of sterilization services in the accredited private/NGO sector. However the accredited private/NGO facility is bound to provide the services free to such an acceptor.

10. As against the existing scheme of paying only to the accredited social health activist (ASHA)/Anganwadi workers (AWWs), it has been approved that whoever, whether from government sector or from the community, motivate/NGO facility is bound to provide the services free to such an acceptor.
11. A self-motivated client is also entitled to the compensation earmarked for the motivator both in the public and accredited private/NGO sector.
12. In states where lady health visitors (LHVs) and auxillary nursing midwives (ANMs) are manning the services in the camps in place of the regular staff nurse, the component earmarked for Staff Nurse may be paid to the LHV/ANMs.
13. In the camp situation where the tubectomy cases are being conducted under local anesthesia administered by the operating surgeon himself in the absence of an anesthetist, the component earmarked for the anesthetist may be paid to operating surgeon.

Guidelines for Sterilization Done at Accredited Private Centre/NGO

A. **In High Focus States (HFS):** Vasectomy and Tubectomy in all categories

B. **Non High Focus States (NHFS):** Vasectomy for all categories and tubectomy for BPL/SC/ST only

1. The state should **accredited the private facility/NGO and empanel its doctors** for providing sterilization services as **per the qualification requirement and criteria for accreditation** (please refer to the manual on slandered for female and male sterilization services, Oct. 6, GOI-Red Book).
2. A minimum of two private facilities (can be more) should be accredited per block for provision of these services. If the block has only one private centre for accreditation the centre from the neighboring blocks could be recognized for this purpose. Accrediting more

private facilities bring in healthy competition thereby ensuring quality services.

3. An amount of Rs. 1500 instead of the existing Rs. 800 would be available for vasectomy and tubectomy services in these private centres. Out of this accredited private facilities would receive Rs. 1300 for each case of male sterilization and Rs. 1350 in each case of female sterilization as against the existing Rs. 630.
4. Rs. 200 for vasectomy and Rs. 150 for tubectomy as against existing Rs. 150 is toward the payment of the motivator ANM/ASHA/AWW/link worker for counseling, motivating and follow up visit of the cases who have undergone sterilization.
5. The package of Rs. 1500 is the Govt. subsidy toward transactional costs of such procedures.
6. No user fee shall be levied on any client.
7. No charges whatsoever for drugs and dressing or other incidental costs should be charged from the client.
8. It is client's choice to go to Govt. or an accredited private centre/NGO facility. However, if the client chooses to go to an accredited private institution; he shall not be entitled to any compensation money, but the client would be entitled to avail of cashless sterilization services at the private/NGO facilities. The client shall also be entitled to the motivator's component if he is self motivated.
9. The upper age limit for men undergoing vasectomy in private institution is 45 years and it is the responsibility of the facility/motivator/ANM/ASHA/AWW/link worker to ensure this.
10. The private/NGOB facility should display prominently its accreditation certificate as well as the range of the services provided and the quantum of compensation for the motivators. It should also display that sterilization services are provided free to all clients (who furnish voucher issued by the competent authority) with no user charges whatsoever levied to the client.

Mode of payment: For availing sterilization services at accredited private/NGO facilities the motivator/ ANM/ASHA /AWW/link worker should facilitate the acceptor in obtaining a voucher from the district CMO's office/DH/SDH/CHC/SC, which should be deposited with private facility providing the service. However, self-motivated client should take the voucher directly from the district CMO's offices and deposit the same with the private facility where the services are to be availed so as to be entitled for the motivator component as well as the sterilization operation. The private facility would then encash the voucher from the District Health Society on production of proof of the sterilization operation. The validity of cases should be ensured by conducting at least 10 per cent sample check and random check by the states. The States Government should devise appropriate mechanism to ensure quality of services, maintenance/monitoring of records and accounting procedure and payment of compensation promptly at the accredited health facilities.

Sterilization Done at Government Institute by Empanelled Private Doctors

The empanelled private provider would receive an amount of Rs.100 per case of vasectomy and Rs. 75 per case of tubectomy in a government facility. This would optimize utilization of government institute where qualified and empanelled service providers are not available for providing sterilization services. In the camp situation where the tubectomy cases are being conducted under local anesthesia administered by the operating surgeon himself in the absence of an anesthetist, the component earmarked for the anesthesiologist may be paid to the operating surgeon. The funds for this would be mated out from the surgeon's and anesthetist's component in the total compensation package for vasectomy and tubectomy, available with the government facility.

Source: www.mohfw.nic.in

4

Family Planning Insurance Scheme

GOVERNMENT OF INDIA
Ministry of Health and Family Welfares
Family Planning Insurance Scheme
Implemented Through
ICICI LOMBARD GENERAL INSURANCE COMPANY
January 2008

Ministry of Health and Family Welfare promotes and encourages the couples to adopt the various methods of family planning and or sterilization. For the promotion of these permanent methods, Govt. introduces, promote and revise various schemes and policies from time to time. Since 1981, Government has been implementing a Centrally Sponsored Scheme to compensate the acceptors of permanent methods of Family Planning, for the loss of wages for the day on which he/she taken the medical facility for undergoing sterilization.

Government is not only providing for cash compensation for permanent methods of family planning but also makes provision for unwanted events or problems to the acceptors of these methods. These unwanted events includes some post operative complications attributable to the procedure of sterilization, incapacitation or sometimes even death (very very rare) of an acceptor of sterilization. Govt. of India provides following compensation:

1. Rs. 50,000 for each case of death.
2. Rs. 30,000 for each case of incapacitation.
3. Rs. 20,000 for each case of cost of treatment of serious post operation complications.

Any liability in excess of the above limit was to be borne by the State/UT/NGO/Voluntary Organization concerned from their own resources.

In the course of time these funds, compensation and policies are revised from time to time. No apportioning of the above amount is admissible for creating a miscellaneous purpose fund for payment of compensation in case of deaths, complications and failures as these are already covered under the National Family Planning Insurance Scheme.

The Hon'ble Supreme Court of India in its Order dated 1-3-2005 in Civil Writ Petition No. 209/2003 (Ramakant Rai V/s Union of India) has, *inter alia*, directed the Union of India and States/UTs for ensuring enforcement of Union Government's Guidelines for conducting sterilization procedures and norms for bringing out uniformity with regard to sterilization procedures by—

1. Creation of panel of Doctors/health facilities for conducting sterilization procedures and laying down of criteria for the empanelment of doctors for conducting sterilization procedures.
2. Laying down of checklist to be followed by every doctor before carrying out sterilization procedure.
3. Laying down of uniform performa for obtaining of the consent of person undergoing sterilization.
4. Setting up of Quality Assurance Committee for ensuring enforcement of pre and post-operative guidelines regarding sterilization procedures.
5. Bringing into effect an insurance policy uniformly in all States for acceptors of sterilizations etc.

Ministry of Health and Family Welfare strictly followed these guidelines directed by Hon'ble Supreme Court and also implemented these in the form of quality assurance in sterilization services and also launched the family planning insurance scheme through ICICI Lombard General Insurance Company.

FAMILY PLANNING INSURANCE SCHEME

Initially there is no provision to cover the indemnity insurance to doctors/health facilities and due to this too many doctors are facing litigation problems regarding the claims of clients for compensation due to failure of sterilization. Government also not made any budgetary provision for compensation to be payable, regarding the failure of sterilization. Due to these certain existing problem, doctors/health facility who are conducting these sterilization operations are dragging their feet.

With a view to do away with the complicated process of payment of ex-gratia to the acceptors of sterilization for treatment of post operative complications, incapacitation or death attributable to the procedure of sterilization, the Family Planning Insurance Scheme was introduced w.e.f. 29th November, 2005 for a period of one year to take care of the cases of failure of sterilization, medical complications or deaths resulting from Sterilization, and also provide indemnity cover to the doctor/health facility performing Sterilization procedure. This scheme is now further renewed and improved w.e.f. 01-01-08 with modification in the limits and payment procedure. The revised package and guidelines are as follows:

Section Coverage Limits

Claims arising out of Sterilization Operation	Amount (Rs.)
Section I	
(1A) Death at hospital/ within seven days of discharge	Rs. 2,00,000
(1B) Death due to sterilization (8th – 30th day from the date of discharge)	Rs. 50,000
(1C) Expenses for Treatment of Medical Complications	Rs. 25,000
(1D) Failure of Sterilization	Rs. 30,000

Section II	
Doctors/Facilities covered for litigations up to 4 cases per year including defence cost	Rs. 2,00,000

Total liability of the Insurance Company shall not exceed Rs. 9 crores in a year under each section.

Section I

- The claim under Sections 1C & 1D shall be paid in the name of beneficiary.
- The name of the spouse and unmarried dependent children should be mentioned on the Consent Form filled by the person while enrolling herself/himself for sterilization operation.
- Death claims shall be settled in favour of the spouse and unmarried dependent children
- In case of no spouse, the payment shall be made to the unmarried dependent children.
- In case of minor dependent children, the payment shall be made through fixed deposit in a Bank Account by the insurer in the name of minor children to be payable on the date of their attaining majority.
- However, the interest accrued shall be paid to the children through their guardian on quarterly basis.
- In case, there are no surviving spouse/unmarried dependent children, the claim shall then be payable to the legal heir of the deceased acceptor.

Section II

All the doctors/health facilities including doctors/health facilities of Central, State, Local-Self Governments, other public sectors and all the empanelled/accredited doctors/health facilities of non-government and private sectors rendering Family Planning Services conducting such operations shall stand indemnified against the claims arising in a court of law, out of failure of sterilization, death or medical complication resulting therefrom up to a maximum amount of Rs. 2 lakh per doctor/health facility per case. The cover would also include the legal costs and actual modality of defending the prosecuted doctor/health facility in Court, which would be borne by the Insurance Company within certain limits. Liability of the Insurance Company under this Section II would be limited to four cases of litigation in respect of every doctor, beyond which the doctor/health facility concerned would be himself/herself responsible for his/her lapse, apart from any other action that may be taken by the Government against the doctor/health facility. The Scheme is uniformly applicable for all States/UTs. Government of India has paid entire premium for the Insurance Policy. States don't have to incur any expenditure under this Scheme. The Insurance Company will make payment against the claims of acceptors of sterilization directly to acceptors or through District Health Office without any hassle.

Operationalisation of Insurance Scheme/Procedure for Claim Settlement

1. The Insurance Policy, called Special Contingency Policy, has all India coverage.
2. The Consent Form filled by the person at the time of enrolling himself/herself for sterilization operation shall be proof of coverage under the scheme.
3. The premium is chargeable on the estimated number of persons undergoing sterilization during the currency of the policy.
4. The premium has been paid by the Government of India at the time of commencement of the policy based on the estimated number of sterilization operations to be conducted and is subject to adjustment at the end of the policy period on the basis of actual number of operations conducted.
5. All persons undergoing sterilization operations in public health facility/accredited health facility in private/NGO sector are covered under Section 1 of the policy.

6. All health facilities accredited by Government and doctors employed/hired/engaged/approved and empanelled by Government for conducting sterilization operations are covered under Section II of the policy.
7. The claims settlement has been decentralized at State levels. The nominated Offices of the Insurance Company will coordinate with existing machinery of the States/UTs. The list of such offices can be obtained from facility provider.
8. For the purpose of verification and medical evaluation of the claim lodged by the beneficiary, the district level Quality Assurance Committee (QAC) shall be responsible for authenticating the claim by certifying the failure of sterilization operation. In case, QAC is not in existence in a district, the claim may be certified by the CMO till such time the QAC is constituted. The proposed constitution of QAC should be obtained from CMO.
9. On receipt of any claim from the acceptor of sterilization under Section 1 of the Policy, the designated official/doctor/health facility shall file the claim papers along with all required documentation through QAC/CMO with the nominated office of Insurance Company as soon as possible and preferably within 30 days, so that the claims are settled at the earliest.
10. Duly completed Claim Form shall be the basis of lodging claim under Section 1 of the policy. The Claim Form shall be duly completed in all respects by the beneficiary and shall be authenticated by the QAC/CMO designated for this purpose.
11. For claims arising due to medical complications following sterilization operation, the QAC shall certify the cost of treatment of such complications. Payment shall be made subject to the limits mentioned in the policy for such cases.

12. In case of claims for death of the patient following sterilization operation, a Death Certificate along with medical report from QAC/CMO certifying the sterilization procedure, as the antecedent cause of death, shall be required.
13. In case of claims for failure of sterilization, the certification from QAC is required along with reasons for failures, if any. All claims arising under this Section shall be accepted from retrospective date i.e. 29th November, 2005, when the risk is first incepted by the insurer under this claims policy and thereafter renewed without break in the period of cover. In case of non-renewal or cancellation of the policy, the claims related to the period of insurance shall be accepted till 180 days thereafter.
14. For claims under Section II of the Policy, the doctor/health facility receiving any legal notice/summons from the Court shall immediately inform the corresponding office of the Insurance Company. The Insurance cover provided under the Policy under Section II, is inclusive of defence costs. For the purpose of claim settlement under Section II of the policy, the designated office shall be Mr. Mayank Misra/Mr. Ritesh Chandra, ICICI Lombard General Insurance Company, Birla Towers, 5th Floor, 25 Barakhamba Road, New Delhi 110 001, Phone 011-6631 0600 and 6631 0800 email ID: ritesh.chandra@icicilombard.com,mayank.misra@ icicibank.com
15. The defense costs incurred by the doctor/health facility shall be reimbursable if incurred in consultation with the Insurance Company, subject to the limits mentioned in the policy for such cases. In such cases, the Insurance Company shall be kept abreast of all the developments of the case.
16. Liability of the Insurance Company under Section II would be limited to four cases of litigation in respect of every doctor or health facility in a year.

17. Stipulated time limit for settlement of claims under Section I of the policy would be 15 working days after submission of claims with all required documents.
18. In case of any claim found untenable or not settled for the claimed amount, the Insurance Company shall communicate reasons to the designated authority of the District/State/UT with a copy to the beneficiary.
19. State Monitoring Committee shall conduct quarterly review of all pending matters including pending claims. State Health Secretary shall head this committee which will be represented by the State Nodal officers from State Government and Insurer.

Limitation of Family Planning Insurance Scheme

The cases of sterilization operations conducted before 29th November, 2005, is not covered under this insurance scheme.

The pending cases in the courts before 29th November, 2005, is also not covered under this insurance scheme.

These cases may be covered under Flexible Funding for State Programmed Implementation Plans (PIPs) and/or Miscellaneous Purpose Contingency Fund created in respective State/UT by apportioning some amount from the grants under the Scheme of Compensation for loss of wages for acceptors of Sterilizations/IUD Insertions.

Source: www.mohfw.nic.in

Sex and Sex Problems

1. Premarital, Marital and Sex Counselling
2. Sex—Different View
3. Masturbation
4. Night Emission or Night Fall
5. Premature Ejaculation (ED)
6. Erectile Dysfunction
7. Viagra (Sildenafil)
8. Female Sexual Disorder
9. Hypoactive Sexual Desire Disorder
10. Sexual Aversion Disorder
11. Female Sexual Arousal Disorder (FSAD)
12. Female Orgasmic Disorders
13. Vaginismus
14. Dyspareunia

1

Premarital, Marital and Sex Counselling

In today's world, busy, isolated and complex life style makes the relations so fragile, that without any proper guidance they may end even on minor issues. Each partner of the couple has his/her own life style, unique behaviour, emotions and expectations from the other partner. Some issues which are very important and significant for their family and social life and some other aspects of marital life which forms the basis and the essence of marital life. Both issues i.e. related to family and social life and another one related to marital or sexual life are equally important. Issues like, communication, compatibility, expectations, conflict resolution, personal adjustment, relation with In-laws and other career plans can be learned and inquired about from the partners, family members and/or by special counselling (like premarital, marital and or psychological counseling). Some delicate issues related to love, intimacy and sexuality are usually little or rarely discussed.

In perspective of Indian population, except metro and sub-metro cities, there is very little trend of ***Premarital and Marital Counselling***. If we carefully look into our family or into our society, we find that newly engaged couples are too busy to make plans for making each of their wedding ceremonies memorable. For couple of months they are too busy in shopping, inviting guests, planning of honeymoon trips and in other social events. They talk for hours and hours on mobiles, and feel at the top of the world. Before wedding and for few months, thereafter, they are happy with their marital life but later due to their individual life styles, negative habits, family and career stresses and other personal issues, living together may become too difficult and it may even lead to divorce. Problems can intrude much more easily than most couples realize.

Premarital and Marital Counselling: This is a special type of counselling which covers the different aspects of life and helps to prepare the couples for a committed life. It enlightens the couples by clearing their views regarding their hidden and undeclared commitments, fears and doubts or other issues which they hesitate to discuss openly but which otherwise are very important for a healthy marital life. The major role of counseling is to detect and resolve the various conflicting issues between couples, develop the power of conflict resolution and personal adjustment.

SEX COUNSELLING

Major issues of marital life are, no-doubt covered by marital counselling but some issues related to the sexuality remains hidden due to hesitation. However, hesitation related to sexual incompatibility is one of the major causes of family breakdown and/or extra marital affairs. Due to gender equality and improved life style, sex for women is now seen as more than a way to become a mother and to create a family. Sex is a basic need of couples and every one expects a healthy sexual relationship with sexual pleasure. Shame, embarrassment and ego are some other factors that make the sexual life questionable and unsatisfactory.

Majority of Indians consider that marriage is the license to sexual activities because marriage is the only acceptable way for sexual fulfillment. Due to social pressure, some individuals lack in sexual experience even at the age of 30 or more. At this age of maturity some people indulge in the fantasies of sex and related activities instead of paying attention to their careers and other activities. Sex is man's strongest instinct and also the basic need of human being.

Maximum people are confused and unaware regarding the sexuality and reproduction. Sexual behaviour is totally different from reproduction; reproduction is basically related to an intercourse for the production of child and is an instinctive behaviour of human being. If we consider sex, it is an art and also a tool to lead a fulfilling and healthy marital life. Sex is also a process that can be learned by time or by experiences. Newly wedded couples may sometimes experience difficulty in performing the sexual activity on the first night or day after the marriage. Some face problems later in life, even after a period of non-problematic sex life.

Sex is a great issue for couples and man's dominance cannot be ruled out for sexually fulfilled and satisfied family life. Problems arise when it is treated as a low priority. Sexual problems in marriage should never be sidelined or made fun off. Importance of sex in marital life totally depends upon each partner and without it, living with the spouse is impossible and may even lead to divorce. Marriage experts agree that healthy sexual activity can save marriages from divorce. Sexual problems, irrespective of the causative factors, frequently cause serious psychological problems such as hostility between the marital partners and even complete breakdown of the marriage itself. The Honorable Supreme Court of India on 21 March 2006 ruled that a wife can seek divorce for husband's sexual incapacity and his failure to consummate the marriage due to such physical handicap.

Male sexual dysfunction is a major cause that directly attacks his sense of manhood and his self-image. A female sexual problem also alters the family life, which can lead to extramarital affairs of their husbands. Majoritie of these problems are psychological and can be solved by proper counselling.

Keeping in the view of the above mentioned aspect, sex counselling covers following problems:

Few Common Queries Regarding (Discussed in Relevant Section)

- Sex
- Sex organs
- Fertility and conception
- Available contraception

Few common sexual problems

- Low sexual desire
- Difficulty in relaxing and enjoying sex
- Obsessive/Compulsive thoughts about sex
- Feeling guilty about sex
- Physical or emotional abuse as a child
- Loss of intimacy in one's relationship
- To be in a painful relationship and thinking about leaving

Some sex related common repulsive emotions

- Embarrassment - shame or guilt about or during sex
- Self-blame, self-consciousness
- Chronic or excessive sadness and/or anger
- Indecisiveness or mental confusion
- Worry, anxiety, obsessive thinking
- Unpleasant feeling, mood swings
- Negativity, pessimism, irritability

And also certain following sexual problems, which have been discussed in the relevant sections of this manual/book:

Male sexual problems and queries

- Masturbation
- Premature Ejaculation
- Erection Difficulties or Erection Dysfunction
- Retarded Ejaculation
- Related to size of Penis

Female sexual problems and queries

- Loss of sexual desire
- Inability to reach orgasm
- Painful intercourse
- Vaginisumus

2

Sex—Different View

Sex! .... Yeah sex.

It is not just a simple word but it encloses the feelings of excitement, lust, love and ultimate accomplishment of life.

In our sexual and/or marital life, meaning of sex is much more than our basic need and or daily routine. Sex is not a 20-20 or one day game, it is a test match and best player must know the basics of sex. **Sex is also a learned behavior and experience makes man perfect.** Sex problems also arise due to the lack of knowledge and imperfection.

It is observed that after few years of marriage sex is only a daily routine of maximum couples. In these couples, man is involved in sex to maintain his manhood and ego and woman to save her family or passively serve her husband.

Sex

Sex is empty and meaningless without the involvement of soul, mind, emotions, blood, heart and/or others parts of body. These are not philosophical words but rather true in scientific language also. Systematic involvement of these aspects during sex in male as well as female is characteristic and is described as *sexual response cycle*. Interestingly if we look carefully, men and women go thrown the same type of responses (stages) at the same time during sex in sexually healthy partners. Sexual response cycle describes the involvement and changing of the patterns of various body parts. In other words the sexual response cycle refers to the sequence of physical and emotional changes that occur as a person becomes sexually aroused and participates in sexually stimulating activities, including masturbation and intercourse.

Sexual Response Cycle

It include following five stages:

1. Sexual desire or libido
2. Sexual excitement or arousal
3. Plateau
4. Orgasm
5. Resolution

1. Sexual Desire or Libido

This is not only 1st stage but the entire sexual activities are dependent upon libido. It is a psychological excitement and also acceptance by soul and it takes few moments to years. It varies from individual to individual and also is dependent upon the intimacy between relationships. Sexual desire is also evoked by following factors:

- Memory
- Fantasy
- Attraction
- Feeling
- Sight
- Physical (contact, smell)

It is observed that sexual desire is maximum in unmarried, single and young boys. They can easily be stimulated by the sight or even dress code of female counterpart. Fantasy is another important factor in these young bloods and this is also a major factor responsible for masturbation.

In case of females this is totally different; except social structure, it is gained and/or increased by the experience. It is also observed during initial few encounters females passively serve to her partner (psychological rape). In women it is also dependent upon intimacy between relationships.

Sexual desire can be easily predicted from the body language and/or the behaviour of an individual.

2. Sexual Excitement or Arousal

These are the initial visible responses of body following sexual desire. The factors which are responsible for the desire also stimulate sexual excitement or arousal. Timing and duration of foreplay also have a significant impact on sexual excitement.

Timing of sexual excitement in males is very small, ranging from few second, to few minutes as compared to females. In teenagers it takes less time as compared to aged person. Woman takes much more time normally to be fully aroused and by the age and experience they may overcome any problem related to excitement or arousal.

Indications of Excitement

For both sexes

- Heart rate and blood pressure increase
- Sexual flush occurs
- Body muscles tense
- Genital and pelvic blood vessels become engorged (vasocongestion)

For men

- Penis becomes rigid and erectile
- Scrotum thickens, and the testes rise closer to the body.

For women

- Vagina becomes lubricated, lengthens and widens.
- Breasts increase in size
- Clitoris swells and enlarges
- Labia thickens and separate

3. Plateau

This is the main stage of sexual performance (sexual act). This is stage of stroking and rubbing during sexual intercourse.

In this stage both partners are fully aroused and its takes around 30 seconds to three minutes.

This is the most pleasurable and exciting stage and leads up to orgasm. The duration of this stage can be enhanced by mutual understanding or by various techniques.

Indications of the Plateau Stage

For both sexes

- Breathing rate, heart rate, and blood pressure further increase
- Sexual flush deepens
- There is a sense of impending orgasm

For men

- Cowper's glands secrete pre-ejaculatory fluid, in the form of 2-3 droplets
- Ejaculation is under control
- The ridge of the glans penis becomes more prominent

For women

- Vagina (outer 1/3 portion) tightens, narrows and swells prepare for orgasm
- Labia continue to swell
- Uterus tips to stand high in the abdomen
- Nipples become larger
- The clitoris slightly withdraws

4. Orgasm

Also known as ultimate accomplishment of sex. It is specific moment at the end of plateau stage or sexual intercourse, when tension of sexual vigour is released. Maximum couples worldwide do sex for getting the orgasmic pleasure of sexual life.

After orgasm, men enter in resolution stage and also a type of refractory period in which he is unable to maintain erection to be ready for another sexual intercourse and/or getting orgasm. Woman are gifted with the quality of *multiple orgasm* in which she can come back in plateau stage immediately after orgasm and ready for getting another orgasmic pleasure in the same sexual act. The intensity of orgasm totally depends upon sexual behaviour of an individual.

Indications of the Orgasm

For both sexes

- Heart rate, breathing, and blood pressure reach their highest peak
- Sexual flush spreads over the body
- Loss of muscle control (spasms).

For men

- *Ejaculation occurs* Emission and Expulsion of semen
- Contractions of: urethra, base of penis and rectal muscles several times around 0.8 second intervals.

For women

- The vagina, uterus, anus, and muscles of the pelvic floor contract five to 12 times at 0.8-second intervals.

5. Resolution

After orgasm human body enters into a stage of resolution. Soul and mind goes into resting phase, body and muscles become relaxed but all these depends upon the sexual behaviour of an individual.

In teenagers or young bloods the duration of resolution is very short, and after just few minutes they go into another excitement stage and get ready for another orgasm.

With the age and sexual experience, the duration of resolution stage increases.

Indications of Resolution

For both sexes

- Increased relaxation, and drowsiness
- Heart rate and blood pressure goes down for few minutes and then recovers
- Sweating is common in various body parts
- Loss of muscle tension

For men

- Penis lightens in color and becomes softer and smaller
- Scrotum relaxes, and the testes drop farther away from the body.

For women

- Vagina relaxes
- Nipples loses their erection and there is decrease in the size of breasts
- Labia returns to normal size and position
- Clitoris resumes its pre arousal position and shrinks slightly
- Cervix opens for few times for movement of sperms for further fertilization
- Blood vessels dilate to drain the pelvic tissues and decrease engorgement

Sex Problems

Sex problems are highly concerned with sexual response cycle and any problems related to sexual response cycle are called sex problems.

In male

1. Masturbation
2. Night Emission
3. Premature Ejaculation
4. Erectile Dysfunction
5. Retarded Ejaculation

In female

1. Hypoactive Sexual Desire Disorder
2. Sexual Aversion Disorder
3. Female Sexual Arousal Disorder
4. Female Orgasmic Disorders

Knowing how your body responds during each phase of the cycle can enhance your relationship and help you pinpoint the cause of sexual problem or dysfunction. Yet some problems are due to physical, psychological, hormonal and anatomical factors.

3

Masturbation

It is for your knowledge that every sexually mature human being masturbates. There's an old joke: 97 per cent of all men and women masturbate — and the other 3 per cent are lying dead.

One should know following points regarding masturbation

- Good for health
- Perfectly normal sexual activity
- Our original sexual activity
- Satisfying for sex psychology
- Useful for stress and anxiety management
- Does not change, the shape and size of genitalia permanently
- Good for those who suffer from premature ejaculation
- Pleasurable and there is nothing wrong with doing it

It is a common practice for man and woman. Except for some modern or westernized societies, it is little prevalent in Indian women and they usually face the problem of orgasm. Masturbation is a healthy practice for those individuals who are not having regular sexual intercourse. Masturbation is the way to learn the experience of physical experience, orgasm and the value of physical relationship. Masturbation is the first step to learn and/or prepare for sexual activities. Sexologists alway prefers masturbation for those who have no feeling regarding their own orgasm after a couple of years of their marriage and they say usually "You can't have good sex with another until you learn to have good sex with yourself".

Masturbation is not recommended for following

- Man who is sub-fertile or having fewer amounts of viable sperms in his semen (Oligozoospermic Patients) and is willing to impregnate his wife. It is recommended to observe sexual abstinence of few days before sexual copulation at the time of ovulation (normally 12-14 days of the MC).
- Pregnant woman having bad obstetric history (frequent miscarriage / premature deliveries).

Excessive Masturbation and its Impact

Healthy practice is masturbation for 2 or 3 times per week, which is normally is enough. Moderate amounts of regular ejaculation are both normal and healthy. Daily masturbation is also a routine for of some teen aged peoples (students and hostlers). But it is observed that some guys usually do it 3-7 times daily and this over practicing can lead to various physical and psychological problems. In common language: too much ejaculation makes a man lethargic and emotionally over sympathetic due to an actual change in body chemistry. Masturbations in young men often is performed when there is a psychological need for emotional fulfillment. This can set a pattern that carries over into adulthood and leads to chronic excessive masturbation. There are following problems which can by arise due to excessive masturbation:

1. Fatigue, even chronic fatigue and feeling tired all the times
2. Absentmindedness
3. Lack of concentration and memory problem
4. Hair loss in male
5. Eye floaters or fuzzy vision
6. Soft / weak erection

7. Lower back pain
8. Stress / Anxiety

But it should be clear that all problemis except hair loss are temporary and only a healthy practice or sexual abstinence can alter the problem. There are certain suggestions which may help you to avoid excessive masturbation.

For Student/Hostlers

- Avoid loneliness
- Avoid looking at pictures or movies that leads to sexual arousal/enjoyment
- Remove/delete pornographic material from your personal computers and hard copies from your room
- Start group study in rooms and use common library facility of the institute
- Busy yourself with games and other cultural activities
- Change your daily routine and or life styles
- Spends some time at the holy places

For Members of Family/Non-hostlers

Except above mentioned suggestion you may also consider following suggestion:

- Share maximum time especially early morning and late evening with your family members
- Busy yourself with household jobs and those related to your profession
- Make a daily routine to visit mandir/masjid/ gurudwara and other holy places.

4

Night Emission or Night Fall

It is an ejaculation during night when an individual is under deep asleep. It is an uncontrolled orgasm, usually accompanied with erotic dream and also known by various names like wet dream, night fall, night discharge, etc. It is also a natural way of releasing sexual tension.

According to the literature man needs to ejaculate from time to time either through sexual encounter or when he is not sexually active through masturbation and if this not done, night emission takes place. It is most common during teenage and early adult years. It is believed that a man can hold an optimum amount of semen and after collection of the maximum amount; it needs to get rid of it.

Common Factors About Night Emission

- Most frequent in teenage and early adulthood.
- 2-3 times per week is quite normal in this age (medical treatment should be avoided).
- Regularly masturbating or having sex reduces the chance of nightfall.
- Discharge does not cause any physical and mental problems.

- Study indicates that sexually mature man have experience of first ejaculation usually through nocturnal emission if he is not practicing other sexual acts like masturbation.

Causal Factors of Night Emission

The exact cause of nocturnal emissions is not known. Some believe that sexual attitude and eating behavior is most commonly associated with this problem. Nocturnal emissions provide a kind of physiological safety valve for sexual tension. It is due to following certain minor factors:

A. Life Style

- Going to bed late in the night and waking up too late in the morning
- Avoiding exercise and morning walk
- Wearing tight under garments
- Living alone in a room
- Getting to bed immediately after meal
- Taking oily, spicy and roasted foodstuffs

B. Sexual Attitude

- Always thinking about opposite sex and sexual activities.
- Watching frequently pornographic movies and other related picture and also studying vulgar literature.

C. Abdominal Problems

- Having worms in the abdomen.
- Indigestion or digestion problems
- Regular abdominal pain
- Reduced diet
- Problems due to gastro esophageal reflux disease (GERD) or gastritis

Problems Associated with Excessive Night Emission

Excess of everything is harmful. There are following certain problems reported with excessive night emission i.e.:

- Psychological depression and guilt
- Anxiety and inability of sexual performance
- Stress and isolated life styles
- Insomnia (lost asleep or sleeplessness)
- Decline in academic achievement
- It may lead to decrease in sperm count
- Inability to produce children
- Memory problems, poor vision/sight
- Severe sexual, physical, mental weakness

Advise to Overcome This Problem

Changing the life style, attitude and treating certain problems associated with digestive system definitely proves better. There are certain following recommendations:

A. Changing Attitude

- Be positive, do positive and think positive
- Spend more time with friends and family members
- Delete all pornographic material from your PC if you have, or discard any vulgar literature
- Be little bit religious
- Express yourself

B. Change Life Style

- Always wear baggy undergarments and night dresses
- Sleep properly (around 8 hours) and at proper time
- Start morning walk, jogging and exercise
- Urinate before sleeping

C. Eating Behavior

- Drink more water
- Eat more vegetables and fruits

- Prefer boiled foodstuffs and salad
- Avoid eating oily, fried and spicy preparation especially all types of meat and paranthas
- Light strolling after meal; avoid sleep at least two hours, after meals

D. Abdominal Problems

- If you are suffering from indigestion, acidity, constipation or having worms in your abdomen consult gastroenterologist.

E. Consult Sexologist

No doubt above mentioned guidelines definitely prove fruitful. But if the problem stays as such, patient should consult an appropriate sexologist. He will better guide about the treatment and awareness that is required for patient.

5

Premature Ejaculation

Premature ejaculation is basically a lack of control over one's ejaculation during sexual intercourse without satisfying his partner. Man is said to be suffering from premature ejaculation if he ejaculates well before the satisfaction of their partner in more than 50 per cent of sexual encounters. If we look at the time window, ejaculation within 1.5 min. from the penetration is also termed as a premature ejaculation. Alfred Kinsey (American Biologist) in the 1950s demonstrated that three quarters of men ejaculate within two minutes of penetration in over half of their sexual encounters.

It is observed that during first sexual encounter adolescents and young men usually experience premature ejaculation and by the course of time and sexual experience they can control over their own ejaculation. Man is highly concerned about premature ejaculation or impotency and this is a major issue related to male sexual activity. Premature ejaculation directly hits the ego of manhood. It is observed that around 90 per cent of these problems are solved by sex counseling/sex therapy.

Premature Ejaculation (PE)

Premature ejaculation is the inability to maintain an erection long enough for mutual satisfaction. Premature ejaculation is divided into primary and secondary forms:

1. Primary Premature Ejaculation

Primary premature ejaculation is a learned behaviour that begins when a male first become sexually active. Like any learned behaviour, it can be unlearned. This form of Primary Ejaculation is psychogenic (as opposed to organic or physical) impotence. (Congenital venous leak is a subset of primary PE and is caused by a congenital venous leak in which the venous drainage system in the penis does not shut down properly.)

2. Secondary Premature Ejaculation

Secondary premature ejaculation occurs when, after years of normal ejaculation, the duration of intercourse grows progressively shorter. Secondary PE is due to physical causes, usually involving the penile arteries, veins, or both.

The Major Causes Related to Premature Ejaculation

- Early negative encounters and subsequently lacking confidence
- Lack of knowledge of female's sensory parts and how to excite his partner
- Lacking proper communication
- Lacking of intimacy
- Lacking proper time of foreplay
- Male selfishness
- Sexual intercourse under tension (family, social and profession related problems)
- Inertness and non-cooperation of female partners
- Erectile Dysfunction
- Few thyroid problems, infection of the prostrate, unusual hormone levels, change in the brain chemicals level (neurotransmitters), abnormal reflex activity of the ejaculatory system and inherited traits.

Treatment of Premature Ejaculation

Premature ejaculation is a physical problem but will develop into a psychological issue if it is left untreated. This is surely a curable problem if you properly explain each and every aspect of your personal life. On the basis of your past history, sexologist or psychological counsellor can help you with this problem. Apart from sex counseling there are following therapies and techniques:

1. Psychological Therapy

Psychotherapy is a treatment of regular counselling of the patients for two or three months. Patients usually call upon the doctors once or twice a week, according to the therapist. Results of the therapy are totally dependent upon dedication, devotion and confidence of the patient towards therapist.

Some psychotherapists also use erection-inducing drugs or placebos to boost up the confidence of patients.

2. Sexual Therapy

- Masturbation an hour or two before sexual encounter increase the erection time.
- Paying more attention to foreplay instead of penetration, excite her to the maximum by sensual touches. At the end enjoy sexual intercourse.
- During sexual intercourse, slow down the process of thrusting, continuously changing the angle or depth of penile penetration will prolong the period of ejaculation

3. Kegel Exercises

- Basically it is an exercise of pubococcygeus (PC) muscles. The PC muscles control the urine and semen and firmness of the organ during erection.
- First of all identify PC muscle during urination, it is found between anus and urethra and then gently squeezing control the urination.
- After identification, contract the muscles tightly holding for 10-15 seconds and repeating the same process for several times. This process should be repeated 2-3 times per day.
- A man can do these exercises anytime and anywhere which enhance the strength of the muscle and subsequently sexual life.

4. The Start Stop Technique

It consists of a series of exercises starting with self-stimulation and ending with intercourse, to gradually increase ejaculatory control. The aim of these exercises is to learn to keep you below the point at which ejaculation seems inevitable for as long as possible.

Avoid all fantasies during the course of exercise, practice following instructions step-wise:

1. Concentrate on your organ and masturbate yourself without any lubricant and stop just before ejaculation. Relax for few minute and repeat the same process for few times without reaching the orgasm. Usually three to four times is enough in this stage.
2. The same process is repeated with a lubricating jelly that heightens the sexual sensation and increase the passion of ejaculation to makes delay more difficult. This process repeated three times at least.
3. Above mentioned two steps help in controlling the orgasm. In third step, masturbate with the help of pelvic thrust rather than using motion of hand (dry). At the climax change the rhythm and/or alter your strokes in such a way that the pressure to ejaculate goes down instead you stop this process. During this process keenly observe the strokes which excites you the most, and which allow you most control. This process is repeated three times at least.
4. This is simply repetition of step one with the help of wife or partner. She will masturbate with her dry hand and ask her to stop just before the orgasm. This process is also repeated three times at least.
5. Repeat step four, but ask your partner to use a lubricant while she masturbates you. This step enhances ejaculation periods. Once you have mastered three consecutive 15-minute sessions, you are ready to try the stop-start technique with intercourse.

6. Now you are ready for intercourse, but not for thrusting. Instead, lie on your back and ask your partner to sit on top of you, with your penis inside her. The best position for delaying ejaculation is with the woman on top. Once you are inside her, ask her to move gently. Neither of you should move. As soon as you feel the urge to come stop her, and when you are ready for her to start again. Again, aim to last for 15 minutes, but if you can't, don't worry; you can start again once you recover your erection, and the second time you will probably have more control. During intercourse, concentrate entirely on yourself.
7. Move on to other positions. It is more difficult to delay -ejaculation with the man on top, so save this until last.

5. Squeeze Technique

Tenderly squeezing the head (Glans Penis) and base of the penis during and/or between the intercourses will also help in delaying the ejaculation. This process can be continued until the couple decides mutually to reach the climax. Regular practice for few days will helps to know the right pressure

6. Medications

- High level of blood serotonin usually delays the ejaculation. The drug which enhance the level of serotonin also used as anti depressant.
- Some food supplement containing 5-HTP, also enhance the level of serotonin.
- Early ejaculation is caused by the nerve supply to the penis being highly strung, resulting in "super sensitivity". In many cases using two condoms, though very clumsy, will lessen the sensitivity.
- Desensitizing creams and gels are available in the market that reduce the sensitivity of the penis and help men reach climax later. Some men also feel that condoms reduce the sensations and, in addition to providing safer sex, help them last longer.

6

Erectile Dysfunction (ED)

It is a physiological and/or psychological condition of a man in which he is unable to develop or maintain an erection that is rigid enough to allow penetration of the vagina, and therefore functional sexual intercourse. This is commonly known by the name of Impotence. Basically person suffering from these diseases loose the rigidity of their penis.

Some men, however, experience constant (chronic), complete erectile dysfunction (impotence), and others, partial or brief erections. Frequent erectile dysfunction can cause emotional and relationship problems, and often leads to diminished self-esteem. It is caused by variety of factors which are enlisted in this topic. Look care fully for these factors and consult accordingly with the concerned person (family doctor, psychologist and sex specialist). It is a curable disease.

Erection Mechanism

Penis is a boneless organ and erection of the same is totally dependent upon the blood flow. An erection occurs when the blood is pumped into the penis and stays there, making it hard.

During sexual imagination, excitement and stimulation some signals from the brain affects the vascular system, blood vessels which supply the penis, causing them to open up with significant blood flow into the penis. The rapid inflow of the blood causes the penis to swell into an erection.

Fully erect penis presses the veins that are present nearer to the skin surface. These veins normally drain the penis of blood. So, the flow of blood out of the penis is also restricted, which enhances the erection. When stimulation ends, or following ejaculation, pressure in the penis decreases, blood is released, and the penis resumes its normal shape.

Erectile Dysfunction is Caused by Following Factors

ED may result from a variety of factors or a combination of factors. These may include psychological, neurological, hormonal and vascular disorders. Certain drugs and chronic diseases, as well as the natural ageing process, may also contribute to ED. For more information, please see causes of erectile dysfunction.

- Age of man
- Emotional disorder, problem in relationship
- Depression and stress
- Lack of frequent erection
- Excessive smoking and alcoholism
- Opium, Opium husk, cocaine, heroin etc. are certain drugs of abuse which may initially stimulate sexual arousal, however they cause erectile dysfunction if used routinely
- Certain diseases like sugar (Diabetes), hypertension and cardiovascular diseases, obesity, increased cholesterol, etc.
- Neurological conditions including and/or arising from dementia, multiple sclerosis, stroke, or spinal cord or back injury
- Pelvic trauma, prostate surgery, previous priapism
- Long drive on bikes may also causes ED but it depends upon the posture and the seat of the bike
- In addition, many common medicines—blood pressure drugs, antihistamines, antidepressants particularly SSRIs, tranquilizers, appetite suppressants, diuretics,

and cimetidine (an ulcer drug)—can produce ED as a side effect.

Diagnosis of Erectile Dysfunction

Diagnosis of erectile dysfunction should always be done in a proper and systematic pattern which avoids excessive diagnostic charges, as well as the psychological tensions. First step of the diagnosis is taking a proper medical history of the patient.

- Medical and sexual histories help define the degree and nature of impotence
- A medical history can disclose the disease as well as the treatment which may be responsible for ED
- A medical history can help in the selection of particular test
- A history of using certain prescription drugs or illegal drugs can suggest a chemical cause. Drug effects accounts for 25 per cent of the cases of impotence. Cutting back on or substituting certain medications often can alleviate the problem

After taking medical history of the patients, following tests should be done, step by step, on the basis of the requirements.

1. Psychological Examinations
2. Physical Examinations
3. Biochemical Examinations
4. Biophysical Examinations

1. Psychological Examinations

A psychological examination is just like an interview of the patients to find out the reason for the same by filling some questionnaire provided by the therapist or the doctors. Psychological examination or questionnaire basically relates to the diagnosis of certain following problems:

- Doubt on sexual performance (it is usually observed in the young patient and in those who are used to seeing the pornographic material)

- Relationship problems (lack of intimacy, mental acceptance or marriage under social pressures)
- Depression
- Premarital relationship
- Nature of Job as well as work burden

The man's sexual partner must also be interviewed to determine expectations and perceptions encountered during sexual intercourse. Also, sexual dysfunction can be as a result of relationship problem.

Commonly, boys and newly wedded young men have problems of erectile dysfunction. They may suffer from psychological complications, if they are waking up in the morning with fully erectile penis and have full erection during masturbation physical cause can be ruled out. They are advised to consult psychiatrist rather than a physician.

The Difference Between Psychological and Physiological ED

Psychological ED	Physiological ED
Erection is present at the time of wakeup (Morning Time)	Morning erection is absent
Suddenly looses the erection	Gradually looses the erection
Complete immediate loss	Incremental progression
Proper self-masturbation	During self-masturbation feeling of the problem of erection
Varies with partner and circumstance	Lack of erections even under most sexually stimulating circumstances

2. Physical Examinations

Some physical tests before clinical diagnosis are essential.

1. Keen examination of abnormal sexual behavior and some secondary sexual characteristics (breast enlargement, pattern of hair, voice, fetish appearance) caused by endocrinological disturbances.
2. Examination of blood pressure and pulse rate of the patients.

3. Sensitivity of penis by touching, preferably by partner to rule out the nervous system involvement.
4. Abnormal secondary sex characteristics, such as hair pattern or breast enlargement, can point to the hormonal problems, which would mean that the endocrine system is involved.
5. Shape of the penis (bends or curves) at the time of full erection may be due to Peyronie's disease, etc.

Peyronie's Disease

At the time of erection if the patient encounters the following problems he might be suffering from PD and is advised to consult specialized urologist instead of general physician.

Excited male usually feels pain, cord like region, hardened along with the abnormal curvature of the penis. Some other problems like narrow and short size of the penis, fibrosis in some elastic tissues of the body, such as on the hand or foot is also associated with this disease.

Sexual encounter is usually painful and difficult.

3. Biochemical Examinations

Several laboratory tests can help diagnose ED. Tests for systemic diseases include blood counts, urinalysis, lipid profile, and measurements of creatinine and liver enzymes. Measuring the amount of free testosterone in the blood can yield information about problems with the endocrine system and is indicated especially in patients with decreased sexual desire.

a. Tests of Blood

- *Glucose test:* This is a common cause of ED.
- *Hemoglobin:* Diagnosis of anemia, which is related with fatigueness and which is also responsible for erectile dysfunction.
- *Complete blood count (CBC):* Diagnosis of anemia, anemia is related with fatigueness and which is also responsible for erectile dysfunction.

- *Lipid Profile:* Monitor the level of LDL, associated with hardening of the arteries and poor blood supply.
- *Kidney/Liver functional test:* Liver and kidney disease can create hormonal imbalances. Blood tests for liver function involve analysis of enzymes and serum creatinine levels, which are indicators of kidney efficiency.
- *Thyroid function tests*: Deficiency of this hormone may also contribute to impotence because they regulate metabolism and the production of sex hormones.
- *Testosterone Estimation:* Male sexual hormone is responsible for all the sexual activity and manhood. If they are persistently low, an endocrinologist (hormone specialist) should be consulted.

b. Urine Analysis

- Protein (Albumin): Related to kidney dysfunction
- Sugar: Related to sugar (diabetes mellitus) induced erectile dysfunction
- Testosterone hormone

4. Biophysical Examinations

Nocturnal Penile Tumescence (NPT)

After psychological as well as biochemical examinations, if there is still any doubt regarding psychological reason, due to the doubt upon patients tendency of hiding any information, NPT is done. During sleep every man experiences erection four or five times during night. This test only monitors nocturnal erection with other useful information regarding erection. In this test patients are fitted with an elastic device around the penis during sleep; the device detects changes in girth and relays the information to a computer for later analysis. If nocturnal tumescence is detected, then the E.D. is presumed to be due to a psychosomatic illness such as sexual anxiety; if not, then it is presumed to be due to a physiological cause.

Bulbocavernosus Reflex

This is a very simple test that helps to assess the nerve sensations in the penis. You can check it yourself; if you find a tight or contracted anus after squeezing the head of your penis it means your penile nerve is normal. This contraction may be delayed or absent if nerve function is not normal.

Penile Biothesiometry

This method also detects the nerve damage in the penis with the help of instruments. Electromagnetic vibrations are used to detect and measure penile sensitivity and nerve function.

Duplex Ultrasound

A duplex ultrasound is a device to detect blood movements and speed of flow in the arteries and veins.

This test helps to determine whether erectile dysfunction may be caused by atherosclerosis, scarring of erectile tissue, or a leaky vein. A number of disease processes of the penis including Peyronie's disease, priapism, penile fractures and tumors are clearly visualized with ultrasound.

This is helpful for the assessment of the potency, cavernosal arteries in the penile flaccid state can give sufficient clinical information without the use of intracavernosal injection of vasodilatory drugs.

Typically, an injection of prostaglandin-E(1) will be given to cause an erection, after which the ultrasound will record penile blood flow and blood pressure. These recordings are compared to measurements taken when the penis is soft.

Due to indirect vascular imaging and a high percentage of false negative diagnoses of vasculogenic ED, are some of the major pitfalls of this diagnosis which may significantly affect the subsequent treatment.

Treatment of Erectile Dysfunction

There are several ways to treat impotency. Not every method is right for every person, and you may need to take a trial and error approach. Some of the methods are:

1. Psychotherapy
2. Mechanical Devices

3. Drug Therapy
4. Surgery in severe cases

1. Psychotherapy

Psychotherapy is a treatment of regular counselling of the patients for two or three months. Patients usually call upon the doctors once or twice a week, according to the therapist. Results of the therapy are totally dependent upon dedication, devotion and confidence of the patient toward therapist.

Some psychotherapists also use erection-inducing drugs or placebos to boost up the confidence of patients.

2. Mechanical Devices

There are a number of devices that can help men to achieve a better erection and to have successful sex.

Vacuum Pumps or Penis Pump

After pills this device is most popular and highly recommended for the treatment of erectile dysfunction. This technique has following advantages:

- Highly economic
- Highly safe
- Easy to use
- Can be used by everyone
- Enhance confidence in psychological patients
- Highly successful and also satisfactory method even when compared to oral pills
- Also used in conjugation with other therapies and enhance the sexual pleasure
- It is also beneficial for those patients who are suffering from small organ size problems

Even when the cause of ED is hypertension, diabetes, or prostate, the erectile dysfunction vacuum pump may be suitable.

Vibrators

These instruments are frequently used in IVF or IUI clinic for artificial ejaculation. Vibrators are highly effective for those who are suffering from spinal injuries, these person not only achieve an orgasm but are also helpful in conception.

Rings: These are known as penile rings, that blocks the penile veins and subsequently help in preventing the blood flow out of the penis and hence maintain the rigidity and erect state of the penis.

These are also used after the vacuum therapy to maintain the rigidity. To enhance the sexual enjoyment some condoms are available fitted with penile rings. And some vibrating rings are also available in commercial market too.

3. Drug Therapy

Pills

There are some oral pills which are very famous among the people. It is also reported that normal people also try these pills to enhance their sexual enjoyments. Usually they are not suited for every patient but they do work for the majority of the patients.

These pills are available under various brand names and contain sildenafil or tadalafil or vardenafil salts or other specific regime (salt). A highly popular, Viagra tablet, contains sildenafil citrate salt.

Facts About These Pills

- These drugs help in the erection and not in stimulation.
- Safe and effective if taken as a medicine as prescribed by doctor.
- People who are suffering from heart problems should consult with physician before using these pills.
- It reacts with some medicines, and may have adverse effects. It should be used under strict guidance in those suffering from some disease or taking some other type of medicine.
- Viagra should be taken on an empty stomach 30 to 60 minutes prior to the desired time of effect.
- Vardenafil can be taken, with or without an empty stomach, 30 to 60 minutes prior to sex.

- Side effects include flushing, headaches, nasal congestion or runny nose, indigestion, dizziness, stomach discomfort after meals are very common.

Injections and Urethral Pellets (Muse)

Due to increasing availability of oral drugs, injections are not very popular and are also painful to use. Drugs such as papaverine, phentolamine and alprostadil (marketed as PGE-1, prostaglandin-E1, Alprostadil, Caverject, Edex, Prostin VR etc.) are injected into the penis, causing it to become engorged with blood due to the widening the blood vessels. However sometimes they may cause priapism (persistent erection).

Alprostadil is also available in the form of transurethral pellets or in the form of gel or cream to be applied to the head of the penis (glans penis).

4. Surgery

ED patient are sometimes referred surgical operation for to following purpose

- Curing the blood leakage from penile veins and also blocking off the vein and reconstructing the arteries to increase blood flow into the penis.
- Implantation of mechanical device into the penis in severe cases.

The mechanical devices implanted into the penis, known as prostheses. Prostheses come in either a semi-rigid form or as an inflatable device. Most men prefer the placement of the inflatable penile prosthesis, which consists of a pump that contains the inflation and deflation mechanism.

Some malleable implants usually consist only paired rods, which are inserted surgically into the corpora cavernosa and insertion does not increase the width of the penis.

7

Viagra (Sildenafil)

Viagra is also known by the name of "Blue Pill", "Magic Pill", "Vitamin V", and some other local nicknames. Viagra or Sildenafil citrate is the world's first drug used for male impotence or erectile dysfunction and today Viagra is a well-known drug throughout the world.

It is the miracle medicine for the person who is suffering from poor erection and/or erectile dysfunction. Basically, it helps in maintaining proper erection during copulation and enhances the sexual satisfaction rate of their partner.

Erectile Dysfunction (ED) is a common problem of a man who has crossed the age of 40. Some men complain of not getting an erection at all, few can get it but it's not hard enough for sex while others get a hard erection but lose it before or during the peak time of sexual intercourse. Viagra brings about a stronger and longer penis erection.

Viagra Tablet

Sildenafil Citrate is the main salt of the tablet

Color: Blue

Shape: Film-coated rounded-diamond-shaped tablets

Dosage: Generally available in three dosages i.e. 25, 50 and 100 mg

In addition to the active ingredient, sildenafil citrate, each tablet contains the following inactive ingredients:

microcrystalline cellulose, hypromellose, lactose, triacetin, anhydrous dibasic calcium phosphate, croscarmellose sodium, magnesium stearate, titanium dioxide, and FD & C Blue #2 Aluminum Lake

Dosage

On the basis of medical condition and response to therapies the dosage of drug is decided by the doctor or pharmacist. *Interactions of the drug are also an important factor for deciding the dosage of drug.*

If patient is not using any type of medicine and won't like to consult with the physician, he may start with the lowest dosage of the medicine and increase the dosage as may be required. Directly using high dosage pill may create some physiological problems like severe dizziness, fainting and/or prolonged erection.

It is also suggested to carefully read the patient Information leaflet provided by the manufacturer of pills before you start taking Viagra. If you have any questions, consult your doctor or pharmacist.

Basic Information Regarding the Oral Uses of Viagra (Sildenafil)

- As per one's requirement, taken orally at least 30 minutes, but not more than 4 hours before sexual activity. 1 hour before is the most effective.
- Viagra can work in as little as 14 minutes
- Low fat diet is usually recommended to those patients because a high fat meal may delay the time of onset of action of this drug.
- Try to avoid eating grapefruit or drinking grapefruit juice during the course of Viagra.
- Do not take more often than once daily, and take as directed.

Women: Viagra is neither approved nor recommended for use in women. Therefore, women should not take Viagra under any circumstances. However, for women on certain antidepressants, Viagra may be the key to achieving orgasm, at least according to a recent study published in the Journal of the American Medical Association.

The study was conducted on women taking SSRIs (like Prozac or Paxil) to treat their depression. During the study, these women were asked to take a pill just prior to engaging in sexual activity. For half of the women, the pill was Viagra, and for half it was a Placebo.

Older Men: Men older than 65 are very sensitive to the effects of Viagra, hence they are started on a smaller dose (25 mg) and dose is increased if tolerated as per requirements.

Medical Conditions or Physical Problems: A person should consult with his doctor if he is suffering from following certain physical problems:

- Arrhythmias (irregular heartbeat)
- High blood pressure or low blood pressure
- Heart or blood diseases
- Coronary artery disease
- Heart attack or a history of it (within the last 6 months)
- Stroke or a history of it (within the last 6 months)—Chance of problems reccurring may be increased
- Conditions causing thickened blood or slower blood flow, including leukemia, multiple myeloma (tumors of the bone marrow, or polycythemia, sickle cell disease, and thrombocythemia (blood problems)
- Bleeding problems
- Retinitis pigmentosa (disorder of the retina)
- Kidney problems (severe)
- Liver problems (severe) - Lower starting doses may be used and dose increased as needed and tolerated.
- Priapism (prolonged erection) or a history of priapism
- Abnormal penis, including curved penis and birth defects of the penis
- HIV/AIDS: Certain HIV drugs may interact with Viagra

Other Medicines: There are few drugs which alter the way Viagra works in the body and vice versa. These drugs interact in such a way that they could cause harm or severe illness. Therefore, these drugs are not recommended for use while taking Viagra. The following is a list of drugs your doctor needs to be made aware of before taking Viagra.

Protease inhibitors drugs like Crixivan, Invirase, Norvir, Viracept, Fortovase, Agenerase, Lopinavir, increase the amount of Viagra in one's blood and prolong the action of Viagra. Men on protease inhibitors should start with a dose of 25 mg and at most use 50 mg.

- Cimetidine (Tagamet): Used by ulcer patients
- Erythromycin (E.E.S. or Ery-Tab): Antibiotic medicine
- Itraconazole (Sporanox): Anti-fungal medicine
- Ketaconazole (Nizoral): Anti-fungal medicine
- Mibefradil (Posicor): This may enhance the unwanted effects of sildenafil, unless lower starting doses of sildenafil are used.
- Nitrates/Nitroglycerin (Nitrostat or Transderm-Nitro): Nitrates excessively lower the blood pressure when used with Sildenafil.

Action Mechanism of Viagra (Sildenafil)

At the time of sexual arousal, brain provides the signal to NANC (Nonadrenergic-Noncholinergic) cells in the penis to produce nitric oxide, which stimulates the production of cGMP (cyclic Guanosine Monophosphate). cGMP starts relaxing and dilating the penile arteries with blood, and the man gets a full erection. An enzyme, PDE-5(Phosphodiesterase-5) which is specially found in penis, degrades the cGMP and reduces the erection.

Viagra has an anti-PDE-5 property and it eliminates the PDE-5 in the penis so that the cGMP builds up instead of getting decomposed by the PDE-5. cGMP builds up in the penis and has a larger effect on the artery walls. The greater the amount of cGMP the greater the blood flow, and the greater the blood flow the greater the degree of the erection.

Side Effects of Viagra (Sildenafil)

Usually every drug has some side effects. The drug reaches each and every part of the organ/body through blood circulation and may affect it unintentionally.

Some side effects are common and are seen initially when the treatment is started and/or observed at higher dosage. Few other are rare side effects which depend upon the body response of individual or other physical factors related to health.

Common Side-effects

- Facial flushing
- Mild headache and/or hangout
- Nasal congestion
- Abdominal problem after taking meals

Less Common Side-effects

- Vision problems like, blurred vision, color vision, or sensitivity to light (*Due to presence of PDE-6 enzymes in these cells*).
- Following Urinal problems
  - Painful urination/micturation
  - Change in the colour of urine (Dark reddish or brownish)
  - Increased frequency of urination/micturation
  - Mild to severe pain in urinary bladder (Abdominal pain)
- Dizziness
- Loose motions

Rare Side-effects

- Following eye related problems
  - Swelling, Redness and/or burning sensation of the eye
  - Bleeding in the eye
  - Decreased or double vision

  - At higher dose acute blindness may occur
- Convulsions (seizures)
- Uneasy, nervousness, anxiety
- Prolonged, painful, or inappropriate erection of penis

It is a boon for men with erectile dysfunction if it is used properly and appropriately, according to prescription. Before starting to take these blue pills one should properly remember every aspect i.e. dosage of drug, interaction of with other medicines and side effects of the same.

Substitutes of Viagra

Sildenafil or Viagra is a chemical that blocks the activity of a special enzyme PDE-5 which is essential for proper erection as well as maintaining the same. Any other chemical that has the same properties also acts as a substitute of Viagra for example, Cialis (tadalafil) and Levitra (vardenafil).

Getting and maintaining the erection during sexual activity is a highly sensitive issue for aged men and these drugs hold the promise. These drugs have similar action mechanism but they differ in few side effects

- Colour-vision is a common problem caused by Viagra only (In few cases).
- Muscle ache is observed in the patient who uses Cialis (Tadalafil).
- Viagra and Levitra act only for few hours (2 to 5 hours and after that they disappear from blood circulation).
- Cialis acts for comparatively longer duration and its effect is observed for more than one day.

Note: ***These drugs act directly upon the enzyme PDE-5 which is found only in penile arteries.***

Source: http://about.com
http://health.howstuffworks.com

8

Female Sexual Disorders

Usually females are unaware of the sexual problems and suffer from various types of sexual disorders. It is observed that female's sex problems are generally underestimated because it is usually considered that sex performance is totally dependent upon male partners.

Except some physical, sexual or gynecological problems females are rarely aware and/or consult for those problems. Another key factor is that *males also underestimate female sexual problems*. Due to lack of *knowledge and/or exposure* of females in our society, it is well known fact that maximum woman are unaware about orgasm, excitement or even to sexual desire and this is the key of some sex problems.

The early married females (early teen age), and the other college and school going girls, suffer from the problems related to the orgasm, desire and excitement but may tend to decrease with age and experience. Women with low sexual activity are at a higher risk for low desire and arousal problems.

Now, in the recent past few years people are accepting the fact that sexuality plays a crucial role not only in procreation but also for pleasure. This ideology in the individual leads to one's proper involvement to identify the factors that affects their sexual life. Following are some problems which are dominantly prevalent in sexually mature women:

1. Non-physical

- Hypoactive Sexual Desire Disorder
- Sexual Aversion Disorder
- Female Sexual Arousal Disorder
- Female Orgasmic Disorders

2. Physical

- Dyspareunia
- Vaginismus

Key Facts About Sex Problems

- Female sex problems usually decrease with age except physiological ones.
- Unmarried and or newly married women are more likely to have orgasm difficulties.
- Prevalence is the same for women who report same sex activity as those who do not.

Factors Contributing to Female Sexual Dysfunction

Psychosexual

- Personal, sexual and emotional distress
- Low level of sexual self-confidence or performance anxiety
- Diminished affection or attraction toward partners
- Loss of intimate feelings towards partner
- Lack of sexual education
- Inadequate/delayed psychosexual development
- Unpleasant/humiliating sexual encounters or experiences
- Previous negative sexual experiences: sexual compulsion, violence, or abuse
- Affective disorders (dysthymia, depression, mania) and anxiety disorders
- Unaddressed affective disorders (depression and/or anxiety)

- Inadequate coping strategies (highly sensitive and emotional)
- Body image concerns and increased body changes (wrinkles, body shape/weight, muscle tone)
- Postpartum depression
- Negative perception of menopause-associated changes

Contextual

- Ethnic/religious/cultural messages, expectations and constraints regarding sexuality
- Constant personal conflict with partner or others
- Partner's general health or sexual problems or concerns
- Environmental constraints (lack of privacy, lack of time)
- Life-stage stressors (e.g. child's diseases, divorce, separation, partner infidelity)
- Social ambivalence towards sexual activity, when separated from reproduction or marriage
- Relationship discord
- Negative social attitudes towards female contraception
- Low socioeconomic status/reduced access to medical care and facilities
- Lack of access to adequate care
- Loss or death of close friends or family members
- Lack of access to medical/psychosocial treatment and facilities
- Economic difficulties

Biological

- Individual suffering from endocrinological problems like hypoandrogenism, hypoestrogenism, hyperprolactinemia, adrenal dysfunction, thyroid dysfunction, diabetes etc.

- Chronic diseases related to cardiovascular, neurological or psychiatric systems
- Current pharmacologic treatment, affects of drug therapy on bioavailability of sex steroids or neurotransmitter levels
- Infertility, unwanted pregnancies, abortion, traumatic delivery with damage of the pelvic floor etc., negative reproductive events
- Sexual problems or disorders:
  - Dyspareunia/chronic pain associated with endometriosis
  - Recurrent vulvovaginitis
  - Cystitis
  - Sexually transmitted diseases
  - Pelvic floor disorders
- Untreated or inadequately treated co-morbidities:
  - Psychiatric: depression, anxiety, phobias
  - Metabolic: diabetes
  - Physical: pelvic floor disorders
  - Urologic: lower urinary tracts symptoms, involuntary leakage of urine, urogenital prolapse,
  - Proctologic: constipation, linear scars at the angles of the mouth of anus and nose (rhagades)
- Contraindications to hormone therapy
- Substance abuse (mainly alcohol and opiates)
- Inadequacy of hormone therapy in ameliorating menopause-associated biologic symptoms
- Extent and severity of menopausal symptoms and impact on well-being
- Age at menopause
  - Premature ovarian failure (POF)-menopause before age 40

    - Premature menopause—menopause between age 40 and 45
- Biologic vs. surgical menopause (especially for premature menopause)
- Surgical menopause
    - Androgen (besides estrogen) loss
    - Associated disorder/disease

9

Hypoactive Sexual Desire Disorder

Lack of sexual fantasies and/or desire of sex in females leads to this hypoactive sexual desire disorder and it is highly common in females, yet males also suffer from this problem. Due to the male aggressiveness during the sexual act and the tendency on the parts of female to passively serve the male partners, this problem may escape early detection. Educational, cultural sociological, diagnostic facility (sex clinic), etc. also have major affects regarding this disorder.

In the romantic married life, low sexual desire may cause a partner to repeatedly feel hurt and rejected, leading to eventual feelings of resentment and promoting eventual emotional distance. Some time it may be a major cause for the separation of couples. No-doubt sex is a miracle for romantic, healthy and sustained married life.

I strongly recommend for these patients to seek the help of professionals for healthy relationship.

Symptoms of HSDD

- Lack of sexual interest.
- Passively serving to her partner during sexual act.
- Highly obedient during sex (In Indian society woman never object but show their opposition by a non cooperative manner during sexual act).

Causes

- Pressurized arranged marriages (previous love affair with guy another than husband, lack of faith, acceptance, affection and communication problems).
- Career consciousness and power struggles.
- Psychological stresses such as depression or paying more attention towards family problems.
- A very restrictive upbringing concerning sex, or negative or traumatic sexual experience.
- Individuals who were victims of childhood sexual abuse and persons whose marriages are lacking in emotional intimacy are particularly at risk.
- Physical problems such as heart disease, or any other disabling disease.
- Certain drugs used as anti-hypertensives, antidepressants and birth control pills some time interfere with sex drive, arousal and orgasm by affecting the balance of sexual hormones and the transmission of chemical messengers.
- Menopause: Reduced estrogen to postmenopausal levels can lead to dryness of the vagina making sex painful which reduces motivation. The gradual decline of the hormones estrogen, progesterone and testosterone together serves to decrease drive.
- Testosterone which is potent inducer of sex drive in male and female also is another major factor for HSDD, reduced testosterone levels may be one of the major reason of reduced libido. It has been argued that increasing testosterone levels even in those without low levels may also serve to increase sex drive.
- Another hormone currently under study is MSH (melanocyte stimulating hormone). It has been proposed to be a cause for the increased sex drive experienced in women at the time of ovulation. A recent study on female rats has just been published and shows favourable results. However, the drug is still in

the preclinical testing phase and it will be a long time before we see it in the market (if it ever makes it).

Types of HSDD: There are following two types of HSDD

Primary HSDD

Due to some religious, family, social circumstances or personal attitude, the patient may have never felt much sexual desire or interest, or it may have occurred secondarily when the patient formerly had sexual desire, but no longer has interest.

Some time failure of or painful initial sexual encounter and sexual trauma such as incest, sexual abuse, or rape in early adolescence or pubertal age, etc. can inhibit sexual desire and interest in opposite sex.

Acquired or Secondary HSDD

It occurs after some time of romantic and sexual married life. There are certain following reasons responsible for acquired HSDD:

- Inert and or non-spicy sexual life or partner
- An incompatibility in sexual interest between the sexual partners
- Hormonal deficiencies (testosterone)
- Frequent uses of psychoactive or antihypertensive medications
- Depression
- HSDD may also result from the impairment of sexual function particularly vaginisumus in the female (Erectile dysfunction in male also leads to HSDD in males partner)

Prevention with the Help of Partner

Male partner and or husband can tactfully manage the condition of sexual desire in his partner. Beside their daily routine/job profile and sexual act he can spare some time for his partner for carefully listening and understanding her. It can help with acceptance, affection and in communication problems. It should be noted that sex and affection are not different but affection can help in closeness and increase sexual desire.

After proper communication they may share some romantic view or reading or viewing some romantic play containing some pornographic material also evokes sexual feelings towards their partner.

Therapeutic Options

Psychological Counseling and Sex Therapy

Aware and intelligent partners can easily recognize the existing problems from the above mentioned factor and causes. With the help of partner and psychological counseling and therapy it can be easily treated. Sometimes partners ignore the psychological counseling due to certain excuses or thinking himself to be a good counselor. It can worsen the situation.

For unaware couples, treatment must be individualized—some couples will need relationship or marital therapy prior to focusing directly upon enhancing sexual activity. Lack of the knowledge of sexual education is also a major factor of HSDD, counselor enhances their knowledge and interest with a variety of methods and assignments. It is advised that help of psychological counseling should not be ignored.

Medical Treatment

1. Testosterone Therapy: Testosterone is the major biological factor responsible for libido or sexual drive in both sexes. Testosterone therapy will be useful in the patient having reduced level of testosterone (20 nanograms per deciliter) in the blood. For testosterone estimation, sampling should be done early in the morning (possibly fasting).

2. Change the Medication: As I have already stated above that certain drugs used as anti-hypertensives, antidepressants and birth control pills some time interfere with sex drive, arousal and orgasm by affecting the balance of sexual hormones and the transmission of chemical messengers.

Loss of libido observed in majority of woman using antidepressant (~60 per cent) like Prozac, Zoloft and Paxil. So changing the medication is the best option for these patients.

These should be switched to one that has less of sexual side effects, like Celexa, Wellbutrin, BuSpar, Serzone or Effexor.

Females using birth control pills (hormonal preparation) may change the brand of pills or opt for other option for family planning.

10

Sexual Aversion Disorder

If you or your partner is suffering from following problems:

1. Avoidance of starting and maintaining any sexual relationship.
2. In unavoidable circumstances, try to end every sexual contact as quickly as possible.
3. Individuals may avoid sexual situations or potential sexual partners by covert strategies (e.g. going to sleep early, traveling, neglecting personal appearance, using substances, and being over involved in work, social, or family activities).
4. Not interested to even seeing sex in visual (pornographic movies and literature).
5. An intense aversion to various forms of sexual contact, e.g. caressing, kissing, etc.
6. Active avoidance of genital sexual contact with a sexual partner.
7. Experience panic attacks with extreme anxiety, feelings of terror, faintness, nausea, palpitations, dizziness, and breathing difficulties.
8. The individual reports anxiety, fear or disgust when confronted by a sexual opportunity with a partner.

9. The aversion to genital contact may be focused on a particular aspect of sexual experience (e.g., genital secretions, vaginal penetration).

It means you or your partner is suffering from "**Sexual Aversion Disorders**". The intensity of the individual's reaction when exposed to the aversive stimulus may range from moderate anxiety and lack of pleasure to extreme psychological distress. The impact of sexual avoidance can be seen in the distress of unfulfilled sexual gratification and this avoidance may result in sacrificed relationships and the pain experienced through loss of the enjoyment from sexual gratification and sexual interaction with others.

A sexual aversion basically is a phobia i.e. "Sex Phobia" and has significant impact upon interpersonal relationships. Interestingly phobic avoidance is the fundamental feature of SAD and it is not generated by any physical sexual disability. It is also observed in normal functional female without any physical problems.

According to Kaplan (Sex therapist) person's sexual aversion is either total or situational: "When total phobia is experienced there is panic or revulsion to all erotic sensations, feelings, thoughts and opportunities. Alternatively a person can have a situational phobic response limited to a specific aspect of sex, examples being, genitalia of the opposite sex, sexual secretions, sexual arousal, or a partner rejection." The person with situational phobic state may function sexually and enjoy sex as long as the particular phobia is avoided.

It is important to note that some women who are suffering from aversion disorder have intact libidos and even report pleasure on the rare occasions when they engage in sexual activity (self pleasure by masturbating or as a lesbian).

Type of Sexual Aversion Disorder

Usually patient suffering from aversion rarely disclose their problem or even they may not be aware of this problem. Before marriage patients often seek to avoid any genital contact, even in the context of a gynecologic examination.

By nature they are not willing to share any fantasy/romantic/sexy topics. They also may avoid talking about their aversion to sex in a therapeutic setting. Sexual aversion disorders are of following two types.

Primary Sexual Aversion Disorder

Patients with primary sexual aversion states have always experienced an aversion to sex. Acquisition of anxiety or disgust before the development of healthy sexual interactions with a partner.

Secondary Sexual Aversion Disorder

Patients with the secondary aversion variety have acquired the aversive response after enjoying a period of normal sexual functioning. Acquisition of fear, anxiety or disgust after the development of healthy sexual interactions with a partner.

Major Factors Responsible for Sexual Aversion Disorder

There are following few variables that influence the Sexual Aversion Disorder:

- Some religious and cultural norms associating natural biological functions of sex with the negative connotations of sin and shame. It helps in the perception of this negative connection with natural sexual functions of the mind and body.
- Persistent conflicts from the age of childhood that encompass a combination of separation anxiety, over sensitivity to rejection, and intolerance of criticism.
- Inappropriate alarm response of our body (hypersensitive) towards opposite sex and sexual activity.

Treating Sexual Aversion Disorder

As with diagnosis, treatment of sexual aversion disorder is difficult, largely because patients are often resistant to discussing the disorder. At this time, treatment consists of referral to a psychologist or sexologist for desensitization therapy.

Treatments

I always recommend premarital counseling to all individuals (normal as well as patient) who are going for marriage for a healthy relationship with their life partners. It not only provides the knowledge of sex but also helps in the better understanding, proper communication and conflict resolving power. Marital therapy can be used in the case of relation problems or communication problems between the partners.

Psychological counseling helps in the problems related to sexual abuse or other traumatic experiences. Assignment of psychological counseling helps in reducing the stress and is also helpful in the diagnosis of problems related to stress.

Majority of the problems, arise due to lack of communication or proper understanding. Treatment of the sexual aversion is totally dependent upon the sexual behaviour of patients. Anxiety, fear and stress also play a dominant role in the aversion. Such patients are exposed, little by little, to their fears so that these go away or gradually disappear under professional guidance. Medications like anti-depressants can support the treatment. Psychological treatment that tries to influence the thoughts and feelings about sexual contact is also used.

Panic states can be treated with tricyclic antidepressants, selective serotonin reuptake inhibitors, monoamine oxidase inhibitors, or benzodiazepines.

Patients Using Internet

For females who are suffering from SAD, internet chatting/ cybersex or video conferencing (with Psychologist) are best methods to overcome this problem. It has following benefits:

- Can share / disclose all her problems without the fear of disclosing her own identity.
- Properly share her problem without any hesitation.
- Can explore her view regarding sex.
- Can learn sex techniques with privacy.

- Can feel and enjoy sex.
- Getting an opportunity to interact with opposite sex.
- Enjoy the sexual pleasure without the presence of any partners on own personal computer (PC) and internet.
- The ability to chat and have sexual interaction without commitment to an individual is safer than going to the local bar or gym.
- It boost the self-confidence during sexual act with her partner.
- It makes you confident of yourself.

11

Female Sexual Arousal Disorder (FSAD)

FSAD is the persistent or recurrent inability to attain or maintain sufficient sexual excitement, causing personal distress, which may be expressed as a lack of subjective excitement or genital lubrication/swelling or other somatic responses and inability to attain orgasm or absence or markedly diminished feelings of sexual arousal (sexual excitement and sexual pleasure) from any type of sexual stimulation.

Don't worry; it's a common and also a treatable problem. It is the second most common type of female sexual dysfunction and approximately 20 per cent of women worldwide reports a lack of vaginal lubrication and arousal during sexual stimulation. Postmenopausal woman dominantly suffer from lack of adequate lubrication. Menopause-associated vulvar atrophy can also lead to decreased sensation with decreased arousal. In persistent diabetic females it is usually observed due to the decreased blood flow and may cause an inhibition of lubrication.

Common Factor of FSAD

- Absent or impaired genital sexual arousal
- Vaginal dryness or reduced lubrication

- Reduced sensitivity of nipples, breast and other external genitalia
- Minimum vulval swelling
- Decreased blood flow to the clitoris or vagina
- Reduced sexual sensations and excitement from caressing genitals.
- Persistent, intrusive and uncomfortable feelings of genital arousal without conscious awareness of sexual desire
- Sexual excitement still occurs from other nongenital stimuli (video or erotic fantasies)

Some General Causes of FSAD

- Under stress and depression
- Addiction of alcohol, drugs and or cigarette smoking
- Medications including oral contraceptives, anti-depressants, anti-hypertensives, and tranquilizers
- Menopause is also known to reduce sexual desire
- Reduced levels of Estrogen
- Testosterone levels also affect the libido
- Some time pregnancy or after delivery, sexual desire is found to be reduced
- Systemic problems, such as neurological problems, high blood pressure, diabetes, or hypothyroidism
- Physical problems, such as endometriosis, cystitis, or vaginitis
- Surgical removal of breast (mastectomy) or removal of complete womb due to cancer, may affect her sensation

Treatment

Sex education is necessary for the individual. Change in the pattern of sexual life style is helpful. These are following few tips which help you come out from the problem:

- Accept the problem and empower yourself

- Share the erotic visuals as well pornographic materials
- Enhance the duration of foreplays with sensual massage, without any genital touches
- Even change the bedroom and room should be flooded with dim red light
- Create something new in your successive encounter
- Use of lubricants during act
- Kegel exercises to strengthen the vagina and clitoris

Women may also want to see a sexual therapist for additional help. Psychosocial and relationship issues are critical to successful treatment and both partners are equally responsible for this problem.

Hormonal Treatment

- **Estrogen**: Its deficiency is responsible for vaginal dryness, genital vasocongestion, pain and arousal and hence, the estrogen replacement is the boon for postmenopousal. Estrogen hormone therapy in non menopausal females may sometimes increase the risk of cardiovascular events and breast cancer. Vaginal spray is recommended in these cases but oral estrogen therapy is beneficial to relieve menopause-related vaginal symptoms.
- **Testosterone**: Testosterone therapy in the women who have low levels of this male hormone which is responsible for sex drive and vigour. Sometimes few side effects likes deepening voice, hair growth, and acne may be observed.

Alprostadil: Solution of alprostadil applied to the external genitals (labia, clitoris and surrounding parts) is helpful in improving the sexual response by increasing genital blood flow.

Zestra™: An oil preparation, enhances female sexual pleasure and arousal when applied to the external genitalia including vulva. It enhances the levels of arousal and desire, satisfaction with arousal, genital sensation, the ability to have orgasms, and sexual pleasure.

ArginMax™: A herbal supplement, improves clitoral sensation as well as other parameters of sexual arousal.

Alternative Herbal Remedies: Some Ayurvedic manufacturers recommend that herbal remedy is most beneficial in these cases. This includes, yohimbine, belladonna, gingko, and motherwort but there is no scientific evidence to support them.

Vaginal Lubricants: These are easily available in the local market and reduce vaginal irritation during stimulation and intercourse; and also make the penetration easier.

Some women squirt vitamin E in their vagina to increase lubrication.

Clitoral vacuum pump: These pumps also enhance clitoral engorgement, increase blood flow to the clitoris and vagina, and ultimately improve sexual function and satisfaction in women with FSD (EROS™ Clitoral Therapy device is the only FDA-approved device currently available to treat female arousal disorders).

12

Female Orgasmic Disorder

Female Orgasmic Disorder is described as an inability to achieve orgasm by some women despite adequate and normal sexual arousal. Achievement of orgasm is obtained after the peak of sexual performance (sexual act) or at the climax in the stage of stroking and rubbing during sexual intercourse.

Orgasm is the ultimate of sexual act and every female undergoes sex response cycle. During this cyclic response, sexual desire and sexual excitement stages leads a woman into a stage of plateau and then to an ultimate stage of pleasure called orgasm which is the basic foundation of happy sexual life and satisfaction.

The level of sexual stimulation for orgasm differs from individual to individual. Interestingly, this problem is more common than we anticipate, in context of Indian society. Newly married, unmarried and young females are more commonly affected as compared to elder ones. Women lacking the feeling/knowledge of orgasm are usually more affected. It is also observed that there are some women who never reach a climax. Few achieve it only during masturbation, but never with their partners. In few cases women need clitoris stimulation in addition, to vaginal stimulation, to be able to achieve climax with their partners. In the 3rd and 4th decade of life, women do not need much stimulation to achieve an orgasm.

Facts About Female Orgasmic Disorders (FOD)

1. Frequency is higher in younger (unmarried and newly married) as compared to experienced elder females.
2. Due to religious background and family status, females who never masturbate are highly affected.
3. Unawareness about sex and feeling or test of climax is also a major determining factor of orgasmic disorders.
4. Problem is decreased with increase in the age.
5. Problem may arise due to inadequate genital stimulation.
6. The mood of the partners during intercourse affects female orgasm.
7. Certain problems like premature ejaculation, early ejaculation and also selfishness of the partner is also an important determinant.
8. Mental state of women like household and other family related problems.
9. Some times orgasm becomes a goal for sexual intercourse; this also builds a pressure for the achievement of orgasm, creating anxiety, which is counterproductive.

Physiological Causes of FOD

1. Damaged blood vessels and nerves in the pelvic region.
2. Side effects of certain antipsychotic, antidepressants, narcotics and addictive medication.

Psychological Causes of FOD

1. Fear of loss of self-control during orgasm.
2. Self-image problems.
3. Fear of rejection by partner.
4. Guilt about sex or sexual pleasure.

5. Relationship problems with partner.
6. Emotional abuse, Anxiety, Depression.
7. Fear of becoming pregnant.
8. Past sexual abuse, rape, incest, or other traumatic sexual experience.
9. Life stresses, such as financial worries, job loss, or divorce.
10. A disorder which can result from trauma but can also be acquired through problems within relationships.

Type of FOD

Primary FOD: The disorder can be lifelong or situational. In the former, the woman has never had an orgasm, either through masturbation or with a partner

Secondary FOD: In the latter, the disorder is temporary and may be caused due to unconducive situations.

Treatment of FOD

There is no specific treatment for the disorder. Those with awareness and the readers of this comprehensive book may now be well aware about the certain sexual problems existing in their partners and they can seek help accordingly.

Treatment No. 1

Advice for male partner: Look at the background and certain other aspects of his partner and make her confident about marital and sexual life. Sex is not a sin but is necessary for procreation.

Treatment No. 2

Advice for male partner: Advised to communicate with his partner and to spend more time in foreplay. And try to make her aware about the feeling of orgasm through mutual masturbation or other sexual act.

Treatment No. 3

Advice for male partner: If there is certain other psychological problem get it treated accordingly with the help of suitable counselor or therapist and support her during the counseling procedure.

Treatment No. 4

During sexual intercourse adequate lubrication also plays an important role in orgasm. Dryness can cause painful penetration and hamper sexual pleasure during intercourse; uses of certain lubricants helps make intercourse easier.

Treatment No. 5

Kegel exercises: Toning pelvic muscles with Kegel exercises can help you achieve more intense orgasms. To strengthen these muscles, start and stop your stream of urine several times. The Bermans recommend working up to five sets of 10 contractions a day. The longer you hold the contractions, the stronger your muscles will become.

Treatment No. 6

The best way to achieve orgasm is to remain positive and relax during sexual intercourse and enjoy it rather than work towards the achievement of an orgasm and also try to change sexual behavior or old patterns.

Treatment No. 7

Certain drugs are used in psychological as well as physiological problems and these medications have negative impact on sexual life. Consult with your physician or doctor regarding your sexual problem as well as try to change those medicines (antipsychotic, antidepressants, narcotics and additive medication) which have negative impact on your sexual life.

When orgasmic problems are due to certain physical problem, proper treatment should be taken from experienced doctors or physician.

Treatment No. 8

Masturbatory training may also be helpful in the treatment of female orgasmic disorder.

Treatment No. 9

It is also reported that certain sex hormones which are also responsible for sex drive also helps in getting the climax. Methyltestosterone, a synthetic form of testosterone sold by drug companies is also reported to be beneficial in few cases.

13

Vaginismus

Vaginismus is vaginal tightness, automatically/ involuntarily, causing penetration problem or complete inability to have intercourse. In this case vagina undergoes spasm at the time of foreplay when vagina or vulva is being touched before sexual intercourse and muscles around the vagina contract tightly. In some cases, this can be quite painful and uncomfortable. Sometimes tightness can be so restrictive that the opening to the vagina is 'closed off' altogether and the man is unable to insert his penis.

Some Facts About Vaginismus

- It is a psychological problem.
- It is untrue that women who have vaginismus do not like or want to have sex.
- **The woman does not directly control or 'will' for the tightness to occur.**
- Belief that one's vagina is too small and fear of sex.
- A woman with vaginismus expects pain to come with penetration and so her mind automatically sends a signal to her PC muscles to clamp shut, thus making penetration either impossible or very painful.
- It may be due to sexual trauma like rape, sexual abuse from childhood, fear of sex during puberty,

misconceptions regarding sex, painful first sexual experience and some religious factors of past life.

- Other factors may be: fear of intimacy, fear of pregnancy, guilt concerning intercourse and a woman unconsciously expressing anger towards her partner.
- It is fairly common among women, especially women in their late teens to thirties.
- It is not rare and it is likely that a lot of women will experience it at some time in their life, even if they have had a previous sexual history of enjoyable and painless sex.
- It can disrupt or completely prevent sexual life.
- Vaginismus can cause distress and relationship problems. Newly wedded grooms some time feels rejected from their partner and leads to insecurity in the minds of couples.
- It will also further lead to other psychological perceptions such as; she is a failure because she cannot sexually satisfy her husband.
- It is observed that gynaecological and pelvic examinations are also difficult or impossible sometimes and doctors use anesthetia before examination.
- The severity of vaginismus varies from woman to woman.

Vaginismus and Infertility

Infertility is another side effect of vaginismus. Due to inability of penetration and subsequently ejaculation, most of males are unable to deposit semen in the vagina.

Besides lack of sexual satisfaction, couples are unable to have baby and this is another cause of stress and due to this some marriages also break down. Some couples are quite happy to live together happily without having sexual intercourse, because they love one another. However, they will often seek medical help when they want to plan a family.

Types of Vaginismus

Vaginismus is usually two types:

1. Primary Vaginismus

Female has never enjoyed sexual pleasure due to severe painful intercourse or is unable to allow penetration in the initial encounter. It is observed that some woman suffering from primary vaginismus is unable to wear tampons or allow finger and/or complete pelvic examinations. It sometimes creates unpleasant situations between couples who are unaware of this problem.

2. Secondary Vaginismus

Secondary vaginismus arises after a couple of months or years of successful marriage and/or pleasurable sexual life. In India it is usually observed after childbirth, menopausal condition, some medical complication or due to some traumatic events after marriages.

Advice and Treatment

Vaginismus is a curable problem. Though it is not a serious disease but after marriage it can lead to various psychological, physical as well marital problems if left untreated.

As soon as the woman is aware about this problem, she should consult a physician, sex therapist and or a psychologist.

Sex is a natural, God gifted, right and a basic need of human being. Every one should enjoy this natural phenomenon and there is nothing wrong to achieve the ultimate of sex. You also come into the world by this natural instinct.

During Therapy Following Points should be Considered

- It is curable.
- It requires, will and determination.
- Treatment process is usually long and requires patience.
- If there is depression and/or emotional problem, immediately consult with your therapist.

- It's better if you are seeking the help of professional, because they are good motivators, counselors and helps you in a systematic way.

Treatment for Unmarried Woman

- If there is any psychological problem consult with psychiatrist or counselor.
- Physical treatment and vaginal exercise is sufficient for this problem but consistency should be maintained.
- At the time of exercise woman should be in romantic mood.
- Problem arises due to hypersensitivity of vulvar and/ or vaginal region and basically treatment includes desensitization of these regions.
- Desensitization and vaginal exercise include massaging the vulva and other external genetelia and dilating the vagina regularly.
- It should be done regularly around 20-30 minutes daily.
- Vagina can be dilated with the help of fingers or other similar objects (Dilator) inserted into vagina.
- If vagina is too tight or sensitive some lubricant (saliva, vasleen etc.) may also be applied.
- On the prescription of sex therapist or physician, some anti-depressive (Xanax and Effexor XR) muscle relaxant (diazepam) and anti-anxiety (ativan) drugs may also be used half an hour before dilation.

Note: These drugs have significant side effects on developing fetus, so be careful before use. Both anti-depressants and anti-anxiety medications can reduce sexual desire and decrease lubrification too.

Treatment for Married Woman

- Newly married woman who is suffering from vaginismus should let know the situation to her husband.

- Accept that this is only a psychological problem and will be treated.
- Good partner is really a good motivator and good counselor.
- Create a healthy environment and romantic night at bedroom.
- They can enjoy closeness and share sexual pleasure.
- A good partner helps in dilation and desensitization exercise and should not focus on intercourse.
- Dilate the vagina few minutes before the sexual intercourse.
- Long time foreplay may also relaxe vaginal muscles to some extent.
- Top position is the best for woman in this condition and before intercourse she may also apply some gel, spray containing Lidocaine, novocaine, Vaseline, etc. before sexual intercourse to reduce the pain of intercourse.
- Some muscle relaxant drugs may also be used during intercourse.
- If intercourse is not possible, intelligent couples may also achieve orgasm during mutual masturbation, through foreplay and/or other means of sexual pleasure.

14

Dyspareunia

A persistent pain that occurs only during sexual intercourse or an abnormal pain that occurs during and/or after sexual intercourse. The pain usually appears in the vagina, pelvic region, or the lower back.

Dyspareunia is any pain experienced any time before, during, or following sexual intercourse. The pain may be located in the genitals or within the pelvis. It is not unusual for women, occasionally, to experience pain during intercourse. This is not true dyspareunia.

It should be noted that it is not a disease, but a symptom of various following psychological and/or physical problems:

- Guilt, anxiety, or tension about sex
- Personal distress
- Incomplete sexual arousal
- Forcible coition
- Vaginal dryness
- An allergic reaction to douches, spermicidal agent's, cotton or clothing.
- Inflammation of the area surrounding the vaginal opening
- Urinary tract infections, vaginal yeast infections, or sexually transmitted diseases

- Skin diseases, such as lichen planus and lichen sclerosis, affecting the vaginal area
- A common condition causing thinning of the vaginal lining in postmenopausal women (Atrophic vaginitis)
- A painful condition in which tissue from the uterine lining migrates and grows abnormally inside the pelvis (Endometriosis)
- Side effects of certain drugs likes' tamoxifen (Nolvadex and other brands) and antihistamines
- **Female is frequently aroused but does not reach orgasm. Due to sexual excitement blood is pooled in pelvic area, orgasm releases it quickly. Absence of orgasm delay blood release and creates congestion (Vasocongestion). Vasocongestion can cause an aching pain in the pelvic area that persists for hours after intercourse**

Side Effects

A person who experiences pain during sex may feel embarrassed or ashamed. Dyspareunia can cause problems in relationships or lead to the affected person avoiding relationships altogether.

Dyspareunia and Types of Dyspareunia

Pain may occur before entry, with entry or once the penis is in the vagina. If this problem occurs throughout the sexual life it is called primary dyspareunia. This may be due to certain psychological problems. Secondary dyspareunia arises after a period of normal sexual life and is usually related to certain physical problems. The timing of the pain can provide clues to the etiology.

Entry Dyspareunia (Superficial Dyspareunia)

This is due to following reason:

- Condition of vestibular region and/ or labia.
- Fungal or bacterial infection (vaginitis and vulvar dystrophies).

- Herpes Virus (HSV & HPV) also causes lesions at external genetalia which can be easily identified, may also cause entry dyspareunia.
- Tenderness and sensation at urethra (urinary opening) or other symptoms of urethritis, urethrodiverticulitis or urethral syndrome may also be responsible for the same.
- Vulvodynia that a condition of vulva in which the space of vaginal and urinal pore is so sensitive that just touching the area makes the woman jump with pain.
- A history of pain with entry is most commonly associated with vaginismus and inadequate lubrication from incomplete arousal.
- Atrophic changes from inadequate estrogen levels.

Deep Dyspareunia

This type of pain arises after the penetration and/or during thrusting. It is due to:

- Inadequate lubrication or dryness having significant affect on the friction with penile movement.
- Improper sexual excitement or sexual desire affects the extension of vaginal canal and this leads to discomfort during sexual copulation as well as pain at cervix during thrusting.
- Atrophic changes in the vaginal canal cause the problem during friction.
- Endometriosis, pelvic adhesions and pelvic congestion also cause the dyspareunia in certain cases.
- A minority of women with uterine retroversion and pelvic relaxation have pain.
- Urination with pain and discomfort, frequently urination at the time of night and/or sleeping also causes dyspareunia. Deep pain at or before the time of urination is also observed in few cases having cyst in urinary bladder.

- Dyspareunia may be a part of the initial presentation, which then proceeds to a persistent chronic pain.

Clinical Diagnosis

Carefully taking a history and filling clinical performa which will help in further diagnosis. Then following investigation are performed step-wise if required:

- Inspection of external genitalia
- Ultrasound is also helpful in examination of pelvic and other related organs.
- Colposcope is also helpful in proper examination and biopsy of the labia, vulva, vagina and cervix for internal problems (taking biopsy by miner cut).
- Carefully examining the pelvis as carefully as possible to identify a site or source of the pelvic pain.
- Hormonal test is also helpful in certain hypoactive sexual desire disorders, dryness and post menopausal and related cases.
- Vaginal photoplethysmography is helpful in the diagnosis of vaginal blood flow and engorgement (pooling and swelling of vaginal tissue).
- Vaginal pH test is also helpful in detecting bacterial or fungal infection.
- Sensitivity of clitoris and labia can be measured by biothesiometer.
- At the end of diagnosis, doctor as well as patient should be clear regarding the sites and causes of pain and further problems.

Treatments

There are two types of treatments for the susceptible candidates:

(1) Couple therapy/counseling

(2) Medical treatment

1. Couple Therapy/Counseling

A better counseling is always helpful in creating healthy family life. It not only helps to come out from negative and embarrassed emotions but also improves communication between couples. It is helpful in following problems:

- Fear of sex
- Previous traumatic experiences
- Stress or anxiety regarding sexual intercourse
- Sexual arousal and orgasm problems.

2. Medical Treatment

After taking the history and external examination of genetalia, doctor prescribes medicine and it depends upon the cause of dyspareunia:

- If painful intercourse is due to vaginal dryness, one can apply certain lubricants during intercourse like K-Y jelly, Replens or Astroglide. Increase the duration of foreplay and clitoral stimulation is also useful.
- Some creams or gels, such as Sensua (Viacreme) or Viagel, increase sensitivity of clitoris and assist in achieving orgasm.
- Anti depressant treatment also prescribed by the doctor according to situation. Medications that increase blood flow or relax muscles may be helpful in some cases.
- Antibiotic (a complete dose/dose cycle) should be used if prescribed by doctor for infection in reproductive and urinary tract.
- For yeast and lichen infection (skin Infection of external genetalia and vagina) some creams are available in market (prescribed by doctor).
- Hormonal therapy (Estrogen in the form of pills or cream) is given to the patients suffering from atrophic changes in the vaginal canal.
- Pain due to endometriosis may be cured by medication or through very simple minor surgical operation.

- Some other problems diagnosed through ultrasound or colposcope can be treated accordingly.
- With the help of experienced gynecologist one can diagnose, prescribe medicine and treatment to cure various problem such as Vulvodynia, Vulvo-vestibulitis, Vaginitis, Urethritis, pelvic congestion, pelvic adhesions, pelvic inflammatory disease, Adnexal pathology, Retroverted uterus, Chronic cervicitis, Urethral disorders, etc.

Other Recommendations

- Lubricants such as petroleum jelly should be avoided.
- Pain due to long penetration or during thrusting can be avoided by changing the coital position which reduces the level of penetration as well as thrusting pressure.
- Patience is required because treatment can take several months, especially in those psychologically stressed or in relation to other sexually traumatic cases.

WHO Guidelines

Table 1: Medical Eligibility Criteria for Initiation and Continuation of Combined Ocs/Combined Injections/ Transdermal Patches and Vaginal Rings.

WHO Category 4: Not to be (absolute contraindications)

• Age:> 35 year taking > 35 cigarettes/day • Postpartum: breastfeeding women < 6 weeks' postpartum • Multiple disorders (old age, smoking, diabetes, hypertension) • Rare factor (past thrombin mutations, protein S, protein C, antithrombin deficiencies)	• Cardiovascular disorders ❍ Hypertension (systolic > 160 or diastolic > 100) ❍ Deep vein thrombosis/ pulmonary embolism (DVT/PE) ❍ (Major surgery with prolonged immobilization

WHO Category 3: Risks outweigh advantage

• Age: > 35 years having < 35 cigarettes/day • Postpartum: • Breastfeeding women ❍ 6 weeks to < 6 months ❍ Non-breastfeeding women < 21 days • Multiple disorders (old age, diabetes, smoking, hypertension) (also 4)	• History of hypertension ❍ Where BP can be evaluated ❍ Adequately controlled BP ❍ Systolic 140-159 or diastolic 90-99 • Hyper-lipidaemia

WHO Category 2: Advantages outweigh risks

• Age: <35 years • Obesity: more than 90 kg weight • Cardiovascular disorders ❍ History of hypertension ❍ Family history of DVT/PE	❍ Superficial thrombophlebitis ❍ Hyper-lipidaemia ❍ Uncomplicated cardiovascular disease ❍ Major surgery with prolonged immobilization

WHO Category 1: No restriction of use

• Age: menarche to < 40 year • Parity: nulliparous/parous • Postpartum non-breastfeeding $\geq$ 21 days • Post-abortion: Ist/2nd trimester immediate post-septic abortion	• Past ectopic pregnancy • Cardiovascular disorders ❍ History of hypertension ❍ Varicose veins ❍ Minor surgery

Source: World Health Organization, Medical Eligibility Criteria for Contraceptive Use (3rd Edn) Geneva: WHO, 2004.

Table 2: Medical Eligibility Criteria for Initiation and Continuation of Progestogen-Only Contraceptives (Pills, Injectables and Implants)

Category 4: Not to be used (absolute contraindication)	
• Breast cancer (current or past)	
Category 3 : Risks outweight advantages	
• Breastfeeding (<6 weeks • postpartum) • Cardiovascular disorders • Current DVT/PE • Current ischaemic heart disease • Stroke	• Migraine with aura • Liver disorders ❍ Active viral hepatitis ❍ Severe cirrhosis ❍ Benign/ malignant liver tumours • Drugs that affect liver enzymes (rifampicin and some anticonvulsant, e.g. phenytoin, carbamazepine barbiturates, primidone, topiramate, oxcarbazepine)
The following criteria are special for DMPA/NET injectables	
• Multiple risk factors ❍ Hypertension (systolic > 160 or diastolic > 100)	• Vaginal bleeding suspicious • Diabetes complicated or more than 20 years old.
Category 2: Advantages outweigh risks	
• Past ectopic pregnancy • Multiple risk factors (old age, smoking, diabetes, hyperension) • Cardiovascular disorders ❍ History of hypertension where BP cannot be evaluated ❍ Hypertension ❍ History of DVT/PE ❍ Major surgery with prolonged immobilization ❍ Thrombogenic mutations ❍ Hyper-lipidaemia	• Gynaecological disorders • Vaginal bleeding • Irregular but not heavy • Heavy/ prolonged bleeding • Suspicious • Diabetes ❍ Uncomplicated ❍ Complicated ❍ More than 20 years old
The following criteria are special for DMPA/ NET indictables	
• Menarche from < 18-45 years • Cervical intraepithelial neoplasia (CIN)	Cervical cancer awaiting treatment
Category 1: No restriction of use	

Criteria not mentioned in categories 2-4

In General, Criteria for Women Who Can Use Progestogen-Only Contraceptives Safely and Effectively Include:

• Age: menarche to menopause • Any parity: Nulliparous/multiparous • Breastfeeding> 6 weeks onward • Non-breastfeeding before or after 21 days • Smoking: any age • Obesity	• Hypertension adequately controlled • Varicose veins • DVT/PE • Valvular heart disease • Endometriosis • Uterine fibroids • STDs • HIV/AIDS without ARV (AIDS-related virus) therapy • Thyroid disorders • Antibodies (except griseofulvin)

Source: World Health Organization, Medical Eligibility Criteria for Contraceptive Use (3rd Edn) Geneva: WHO, 2004.

Table 3: Medical Eligibility Criteria for Initiation and Continuation of Intrauterine Devices.

WHO Category 4: Not to be used (absolute contraindications)

• Immediate post-septic abortion • Vaginal bleeding suspicious /unexplained • Malignant trophoblast disease • Cervical cancer • Endometrial cancer • Uterine fibroids with distortion of uterine cavity	• Distorted uterus (congenital on and after operation) • Current pelvic inflammatory disease (PID) • Current STDs • Pelvic tuberculosis
The following criteria are special for LNG IUD only	
• Ovarian cancer • Current breast cancer	

WHO Category 3: Risks outweigh advantages

• Postpartum 48 hours to < 4 weeks • Benign trophoblast disease	• Ovarian cancer • Increased risk of STDs • AIDS
The following criteria are special for LNG IUD only	
• Postpartum breastfeeding or not • Current or history of ischaemic heart disease • Current breast cancer	• Viral hepatitis • Cirrhosis • Liver tumours

WHO Category 2: Advantages outweigh risks

• Age: menarche to <20 years • Parity: nulliparous • Postpartum breastfeeding or not • Post-abortion: second trimester • Complicated valvular heart disease • Vaginal bleeding (heavy and prolonged) • Severe dysmenorrhoea • Endometriosis	• STDs excluding HIV • Vaginitis • HIV infection • Thalassaemia (1 for LNG) • Stickle cell disease (1 for LNG) • Iron deficiency anamia (1 for LNG) • Antiretroviral (ARV) therapy
The following criteria are special for LNG IUD only	
• Hypertension Systolic > 160 or diastolic > 100 • Stroke • Valvular heart disease • Multiple risk factors (e.g. old age, smoking, diabetes, hypertension) • Major surgery with prolonged immobilization	• Cervical intraepithelial neoplasia • Diabetes • Cholecystitis (past/present) • Hyper-lipidaemia

WHO Category 1: *No restriction of use*

Criteria not mentioned in categories 2-4. In general, criteria for women who can use IUDs safely and effectively include: • Smoking: any age, light/heavy smoker • Obesity • Breastfeeding • Ischaemic heart disease • Stroke	• Hypertension • Having antibodies (including rifampicin and griseofulvin) • Post-abortion first trimester • Migraine with or without aura • Diabetes • Thyroid disorders • Liver/gall bladder disease

Source: World Health Organization, Medical Eligibility Criteria for Contraceptive Use (3rd Edn), Geneva, WHO, 2004.

Table 4: Medical Eligibility Criteria for Emergency Contraceptive Pills

Contraindication or delay

- No such condition

WHO Category 2: Caution – extra precautions

• History of severe cardiovascular complications (ischaemic heart disease, cerebrovascular attack or thromboembolism) • Angina pectoris	• Migraine • Severe liver disease
WHO Category 2: *Accept – no reason to prevent use*	
• Breast feeding • History of ectopic pregnancy	• Repeated ECP use

Source: World Health Organization, Medical Eligibility Criteria for Contraceptive Use (3rd Edn), Geneva, WHO, 2004.

Table 5: Medical Eligibility Criteria of Female Sterilization

Contraindications: no permanent contraindications

WHO Category C: *Extra-caution*	
• Young age • Obesity: more than 90 kg weight • Hypertension ❍ Adequately controlled hypertension ❍ Raised BP (systolic 140-159 or diastolic 90-99 mm Hg) • History of ischaemic heart disease • History of cardiovascular accident • Uncomplicated valvular heart disease • Uterine fibroids • Past pelvic inflammatory disease (PID) without subsequent pregnancy • Diabetes without vascular disease	• Hypothyroidism • Mild cirrhosis • Schistosomiasis with fibrosis of liver • Liver tumours • Thalassaemia • Sickle cell disease • Diaphragmatic hernia (laparoscopy may be dangerous) • Kidney disease • Severe nutritional deficiencies • Depressive disorders • Previous abdominal or pelvic surgery
WHO Category D: *Delay the procedure**	
• Pregnancy • Postpartum (7 to < 42 days) • Severe pre-eclampsia/eclampsia • Prolonged rupture of membranes (24 h or more) • Puerperal sepsis • Severe antepartum or postpartum haemorrhage • Severe trauma to the genital tract at the time of delivery • Post-abortion sepsis • Severe post-abortion haemorrhage • Severe genital trauma during abortion • Acute haematometra • Current deep various thrombosis (DVT)/ pulmonary embolism (PE) • Current ischaemic heart disease	• Unexplained vaginal bleeding before evaluation • Malignant gestational trophoblastic disease • Cervical or endometrial or ovarian cancers (as treatment makes a woman sterile) • PID • Sexually transmitted infection (STI) • Current gallbladder disease • Active viral hepatitis • Iron deficiency anaemia (Hb < 7 g/dl) • Local abdominal skin infection • Acute bronchitis or pneumonia • Systemic infection or gastroenteritis • Sterilization concurrent with emergency abdominal surgery or infectious condition

WHO Category S: *Special precaution/ refer client***	
• Postpartum uterine rupture or perforation • Post-abortion uterine perforation • Multiple risk factors for arterial cardiovascular disease (old age, smoking, diabetes mellitus and hypertension) • Raised blood pressure (systolic ≥ 100 mg Hg) • Hypertension with vascular disease • Complicated vascular disease • Endometriosis • AIDS • Known pelvic tuberculosis	• Diabetes with nephropathy/ retinopathy/ neuropathy • Diabetes with other vascular disease or of > 20 year's duration • Hyperthyroidism • Severe cirrhosis • Coagulation disorders • Chronic asthma, bronchitis; emphysema or lung infection • Fixed uterus due to previous surgery or infection • Abdominal wall or umbilical hernia

* Conditions must be treated and resolved before operation.
**Refer to centre with facilities for general an aesthesia and other medical support where an experienced surgeon or staff can perform the procedure.

Source: World Health Organization, Medical Eligibility Criteria for Contraceptive Use (3rd Edn), Geneva: WHO, 2004.

Table 6: Medical Eligibility Criteria of Male Sterilization (Vasectomy)

Contraindications: no permanent contra indicators

WHO Category C: *Require extra cautions*

• Previous scrotal surgery • Young age • Large varicocele (may be repaired during vasectomy) • Large hydrocele (may be repaired during vasectomy)	• Crytorchidism • Diabetes mellitus • Depressive disorders

WHO Category D: *Require delay**

• Local infections • Scrotal skin infection • Active sexually transmitted infection(STI) • Balanitis • Epididymitis or orchitis	• Systemic infections or gastroenteritis • Filariasis/elephantiasis (great difficulty in palpating scrotum and spermatic cord) • Intrascrotal mass (may indicate an underlying dissease)

WHO Category S: *Special precautions/ refer client***

- Inguinal hernia (may be repaired during vasectomy)
- Coagulation disorders
- AIDS

*Conditions must be treated and resolved before operation.
**Refer to centre with facilities are general anaesthesia and other medical support where an experienced surgeon or staff can perform the procedure.

Source: World Health Organization, Medical Eligibility Criteria for Contraceptive Use (3rd Edn.), Geneva: WHO, 2004

DECLARATION

- This is an attempt to make the people aware and to enhance their knowledge regarding the various aspects of reproduction, contraception, family planning and sex.
- Author is not a medical practitioner, therefore, do consult a qualified doctor before adopting any method explained in the book.
- Though due care has been taken while mentioning the various Acts, Rule & Regulations but the author is not responsible for any omission and commission.
- Experience based suggestions from the esteemed readers are invited for the betterment of the book.

Dr. Kuldeep Kaushik
V&PO Romana Albel Singh
Distt. Faridkot (Punjab)
Pin-151204
kaushik.puchd@yahoo.com